D0907952

The 6 Marks of Progressive Christian Worship Music

The 6 Marks of Progressive Christian Worship Music

BRYAN J. SIRCHIO

authorHOUSE®

AuthorHouse™
1663 Liberty Drive
Bloomington, IN 47403
www.authorhouse.com
Phone: 1-800-839-8640

© 2012 by Bryan J. Sirchio. All rights reserved.
P.O. Box 45236, Madison, WI 53744-5236. 1-800-735-0850

www.bryansirchio.com
www.progressivechristianworshipmusic.com
www.6marks.com

Cover Design by Kim Jore
www.riverzen.com

No part of this book may be reproduced, stored in a retrieval system, or transmitted by any means without the written permission of the author.

The Scripture quotations contained herein are from the New Revised Standard Version Bible, copyright 1989, Division of Christian Education of the National Council of Churches of Christ in the U.S.A. Used by permission. All rights reserved.

Published by AuthorHouse   08/20/2012

ISBN: 978-1-4772-4957-4 (sc)
ISBN: 978-1-4772-4956-7 (e)

Library of Congress Control Number: 2012913087

Any people depicted in stock imagery provided by Thinkstock are models, and such images are being used for illustrative purposes only.
Certain stock imagery © Thinkstock.

This book is printed on acid-free paper.

Because of the dynamic nature of the Internet, any web addresses or links contained in this book may have changed since publication and may no longer be valid. The views expressed in this work are solely those of the author and do not necessarily reflect the views of the publisher, and the publisher hereby disclaims any responsibility for them.

CONTENTS

Some Preliminary Words from the Author vii
Introduction: Why I Wrote This Book, and Who I Hope Will
        Read It xiii

Section One: The 6 Marks of Progressive Christian Worship Music

Chapter 1:   Praise, Justice, and the Fullness of Human
           Experience 3
Chapter 2:   Inclusive language.. 8
Chapter 3:   Progressive Theology... 23
Chapter 4:   An Emphasis On Both The Individual And The
           Community 34
Chapter 5:   Emotional Authenticity 42
Chapter 6:   Fresh Images, Ideas, and Language...................... 51

Section Two: Worship, Songs, and Ego Work

Chapter 7:   Worship And The Purpose of Worship Music................. 65
Chapter 8:   Musical Styles And The "Language of the Heart"........... 80
Chapter 9:   Worship, Performance, And Ego Work 92
Chapter 10: Some Thoughts About Worship Songs....................... 102

Section Three: The Bible and More About Progressive Theology

Chapter 11: A Progressive Approach to the Bible 113
Chapter 12: More About Progressive Theology 129
Chapter 13: Some Closing Thoughts and Invitations 157
Chapter 14: Sources of Progressive Christian Worship Music 160

SOME PRELIMINARY WORDS FROM THE AUTHOR

Thanks so much for finding your way to this book!

If you are not at all familiar with me, you may be wondering a bit about my credentials, etc., and what it is that qualifies me to write a book on Progressive Christian Worship Music. In other words, why in the world should you take time to read what I've written?

Well of course you can find out a lot about me by visiting my website, www.bryansirchio.com. Check out lyrics and listen to MP3 clips on the site if you like. Or Google me. You'll find a bunch of links to explore if you're curious to find out more about me and my ministry.

I'd like to confess though that I have ambivalent feelings when it comes to using credentials. It always feels a bit presumptuous to use degrees or achievements in order to try to convince folks that my perspective might be valid. Then again, if I were in your shoes I'd want to know a bit about who has written this book and why.

So I'll just share with you now that I'm a passionate follower of Jesus, a graduate of Duke University with a degree in Religion, and that I got my M.Div. degree at Princeton Theological Seminary. I'm an ordained pastor in the United Church of Christ, and I served two small churches in northern Wisconsin as a solo pastor for 4 years in the mid 1980's.

Since 1987, I've been engaged in a full-time freelance itinerant ministry of music. I founded a company called "Crosswind Music," and this is the organizational umbrella under which I do the business of my ministry and through which I create and publish music and related resources.

I write solo and congregational songs for all ages that help folks explore what it means to be a Christian and to attempt to live in the Way of Christ. I play guitar and piano, and have published about 200 original songs. I've released 13 CDs, 4 songbooks, and 4 study guides based on my music. My songs have also been recorded by several other artists and published in numerous songbooks and Christian education curricula.

I travel around the country offering concerts of my original music, leading worship services, facilitating retreats, providing music, workshops, and keynote addresses for conferences, and consulting with congregations on how to bring fresh vitality and power into worship services.

In 2011, I helped—along with three other nationally known composers and music ministers—to put together an event called "SHIFT: A Musical Retreat for the Progressive Christian Movement." That event has evolved into an ongoing movement, and you can read more about the SHIFT community in this book's final chapter. In short, SHIFT is an attempt to bring progressive Christian pastors and musicians and worship leaders together to define, experience, create, and share Progressive Christian Worship Music.

I have also worked extensively since 1990 with grass roots organizations among the poorest of the poor in Haiti, and have helped to lead two different non-profit organizations that focus on economic justice from a Christian perspective. These organizations (Ministry of Money, now called Faith and Money Network, and Harvest Time) both grew out of the well-known Church of the Saviour in Washington, D.C.

I'm also on the board of directors of a food and education organization called The What If? Foundation. What If? is based in the San Francisco, CA area and provides funds and relational support for a feeding and educational program in Port au Prince, Haiti. Additionally, I'm one of the founders of a group called Haiti Allies in Madison, WI. Haiti Allies also partners with Haitian colleagues to promote education, food for hungry students, and jobs in Haiti. My work among some of the world's most impoverished communities has greatly impacted my life and the music I compose.

I've been privileged to share my ministry of song in well over a thousand different congregations and retreat centers throughout the years, and I have been uniquely privileged to "take the temperature" of the worship life of countless church communities. My work has unfolded primarily in traditional "mainline" Protestant churches (United Church of Christ, Presbyterian, Methodist, Episcopalian, ELCA Lutheran, Moravian, Disciples of Christ, etc.), and also in quite a few Roman Catholic parishes.

My music ministry has been an amazing adventure, and I'm still on the road most weekends sharing my original songs and ministering in one way or another. I am so profoundly blessed to be able to do what I love to do and to make a living doing it. Believe me, I realize what an incredible privilege this is!

Okay, enough about me and what I've done that might establish at least a little bit of credibility when it comes to the area of music and worship. The truth is that even with all my years of experience, I don't consider myself to have any "definitive word" in the area of church music—or anything else for that matter! I'm just a person who has been "out there" for a while now trying to respond to God's call on my life in connection with some musical gifts I've been given.

Most of what I know and what I've learned has come to me through the good old school of hard knocks and trial and error, and now and then by what has "worked" in ways that have surprised, moved, and humbled me. I don't by any means claim to have all the answers, but I have paid close attention to what has been going on in the worship services of the churches I've visited—both when things have seemed vital and alive, and when they have not . . .

After all these years, one thing I do know is that there is a profound hunger in many traditional churches these days for some fresh ways of worshipping God through new music, lyrics, and liturgies that fit who we are as "mainline Christians." This book is my attempt to help describe and define what I think this new music can, and perhaps even *should* be about ("should" is in italics because in general it's a policy of mine to do my best not to "should" on people!).

A few more quick things I'd like to mention here . . .

First, please know that I deliberately created lots of space between paragraphs in the text, and that I also am aware that I broke the text up into paragraphs in ways that are not always "grammatically correct." I did this to make the text easier on readers' eyes and also for a certain effect that I've seen and liked in some recently published books I've read. I find this format especially helpful to those who prefer to download eBooks and read them on digital devises.

Second, I tend to use the terms "mainline church," "traditional church," and "progressive church" somewhat interchangeably throughout the book. I just want you to know that I am well aware that many mainline congregations and clergypersons would not consider themselves to be "progressive Christians" in the ways that I define in the book.

At the same time, mainline clergy who do not necessarily define themselves as progressive often have many of the same problems with "contemporary praise and worship" music that progressive Christian pastors tend to have. I think most mainline clergy will appreciate the substance of the "6 Marks of Progressive Christian Worship Music" even if they do not necessarily resonate with all of my theological reflections as one who refers to himself as a progressive Christian.

Third, I want you to know that while I am obviously embracing and using the word "progressive," I long for a day when labels like "progressive" (or evangelical, conservative, liberal, mainline, traditional, fundamentalist, emerging, etc.) will not be necessary at all. I would like for the word "Christian" to stand for something beautiful and real in and of itself, and not need any qualifying terms. But the simple truth is that "Christian" has come to take on way too much negative baggage at this point in history for it to be able to stand alone and have a chance of pointing people toward what I think it means to be a follower of Jesus.

I even toyed with using the term "post-progressive" in order to underscore my desire to get beyond the need for labels altogether. Labels too often wind up being disrespectful, polarizing, and divisive, and I think many of us are tired of framing conversations in terms of categories that somehow only further an adversarial or dismissive posture.

But "Post-Progressive Christian Worship Music" just didn't have much of a ring to it, and chances are no one would know what I was talking about unless I explained it!

The word "progressive" does communicate well.

It gives folks a pretty good clue as to the kinds of themes that this worship music will reflect. And, the truth is that while I don't want to use any adjective or label in order to put down another "group," I *am* trying to differentiate this new genre of worship music from much of the "praise and worship" music that currently exists in the Christian Music industry. So again, the word progressive helps to establish a particular identity.

That being said, it seems as though more and more Christians are claiming the word "progressive" these days as a way of distinguishing ourselves, and there may be areas of disagreement between some of these groups. There is an exciting movement currently among evangelical (or former or "recovering" evangelical) Christians who tend to come from conservative Christian backgrounds and who now refer to themselves as "progressive Christians." There is also a significant progressive Christian movement among more liberal or mainline Christians.

We might say that some progressive Christians are emerging "from the right," and some "from the left." There may be clashes of sorts as these groups find ourselves in the center of the progressive Christian movement together. Personally, I think it's wonderful and very much of the Holy Spirit that these different groups are finding each other and entering into fresh dialogue.

But it also makes words like "progressive" a bit trickier to use. I have recently seen the words "Convergent" or "Converging Christians" used to refer to this fresh coming together of Christians from evangelical and liberal traditions who are all tired of labels that box us in and create tension between us. I like the word "converging," and I like the conversation out of which this term seems to be springing forth. That's really where my heart is.

As will be obvious, I come more from the more mainline church end of this dialogue. But my earliest church affiliation after my conversion experience at age 17 was in an evangelical Pentecostal congregation. I have great affection and appreciation for these evangelical roots of mine even though I obviously have evolved in a different direction theologically. But I am excited to learn from and work with evangelical brothers and sisters who are asking similar questions and working with similar issues to those addressed in this book.

Thanks again for finding your way to this material, for purchasing it if you did, and please know that I welcome your responses and look forward to being in conversation with you.

And thanks for caring about music, worship, and the Church as much as you do. It means a lot to me that you're invested enough to spend some time thinking deeply about how to best help your congregation sing its faith with integrity, passion, and joy.

Your brother in Christ,

Bryan Sirchio

INTRODUCTION

Why I Wrote This Book, and Who I Hope Will Read It

I'm going to begin this adventure with you by explaining why I decided to take this project on in the first place, and how I'm hoping this resource will be used.

To put it mildly, the number of so-called mainline or traditional Protestant congregations using "contemporary" music in their worship services has exploded in recent decades. There are all kinds of reasons for this, some of which are solid and Spirit-led in my opinion, and some of which are probably questionable at best.

Despite the reasons why congregations have decided to bring more modern music into their worship services, there is often an awkward conversation that eventually takes place between pastors in these churches and the musicians who participate in the "praise and worship bands" (or whatever they choose to call themselves). Here's how things often unfold.

The process often begins with a pastor and/or worship committee of some kind determining that it's time for the church to use more "contemporary music" (all of the labels we could use for this new music have their problems and limitations) in its services of worship. The next step is to find some musicians in the congregation or community who are willing to help lead this new contemporary worship music.

If all goes well, some members or friends of the congregation step forward and a band is formed. So far so good. Hopefully the musicians are decent players, committed to their faith, and committed to the congregation.

Hopefully they also understand that the purpose of this new church band is to help the congregation worship more deeply—and not just a chance for former garage band rock star wanna-be's to be on "stage" again. I know—lots could be said here. We'll pick this particular topic up again later on in the book.

But next comes the hard part. What songs will the band play? Where will they find some good new worship music? There are a few notable exceptions, but most mainline denominations and publishing houses have been extremely slow to respond to the vast numbers of traditional churches now looking for contemporary worship music. So these band members inevitably wind up going to a local "Family Bookstore" or "Bible Bookstore" in search of contemporary "praise and worship" music. Or, more often now, they go online searching for contemporary worship songs.

And they are not disappointed! In fact, they are delighted to find that a multi-billion dollar industry has emerged in more evangelical or fundamentalist circles (again, I wish the labels weren't necessary but I'll trust you know what I mean) in response to the need for contemporary worship music and related resources.

This industry provides everything the worship band could possibly need—CDs, songbooks, accompaniment tracks, videos, lyrics for projection on large screen, downloadable music and lead sheets, etc. After listening to a number of different worship artists and bands, many of which are also stars in the Contemporary Christian Music scene and readily heard on Christian Radio's top 40, some music is purchased and the band excitedly brings these hit Christian worship songs into their more traditional or mainline church worship services.

And then what happens?

Well some folks are usually thrilled. Or at least open and optimistic. They like the music, and they're glad that their church is trying to "get with the times." They're glad to be able to worship God with music that feels less "churchy." They're hopeful that maybe the younger folks in the congregation will think this new music is cool and that it will be attractive to people who are bored with or turned off by hymns that are hundreds of years old.

Chances are there will also be some members of the church who are *not* all that thrilled with this new worship music. They may the not care for the style of the music, or they may struggle with whether or not this music is appropriate for church or "feels like church" or whether or not more up-tempo music with a rock band can be considered "sacred music."

Or perhaps they love classical music and fear that the church is going to become less classy, polished, or sophisticated.

Or maybe some folks are afraid that the hymns they've grown to love and value and to which they have developed great emotional and sentimental (and sometimes theological) ties over a lifetime are in the process of being disrespected or discarded altogether.

There are all kinds of reasons why folks respond to this new music in different ways—some positive, some negative, and some in between. That's all to be expected and anticipated. It's always a tricky thing at best to substantially change the tone, feel, and style of a church's worship service, and it's always a potentially controversial thing to in any way "mess" with the church's music.

THE PASTOR'S AGONY

But there is often at least one person in the congregation who may be quietly developing a case of theological hives, and who may be privately (or sometimes quite obviously!) cringing as he or she attempts to worship God through this more contemporary sounding music—and that is the pastor. There may be others in the congregation in addition to the pastor—people who take their spiritual lives seriously and who would most likely identify themselves as being theologically more "liberal" or "progressive" (again—the labels all have their problems)—who are also having a hard time with this new music.

It's usually not the music that bothers the pastors and the more progressive members of the congregation. Or at least not primarily the music.

Most often it's the words of the songs.

And let's just focus on the pastors for a minute.

Something about the lyrics of many of the hit contemporary Christian worship songs is at best problematic for many clergy persons in mainline denominations. Sometimes the songs are downright offensive theologically to the pastor. Often the problem is rooted in a theological nuance or doctrine that the pastor does not embrace.

Sometimes these contemporary worship songs use too many Christian buzz words or clichés—words or phrases that the pastor deliberately avoids in every other aspect of the liturgy. Often the problem is that the new songs show no sensitivity at all to things like "inclusive language" or the theological challenges of doctrines like "penal substitutionary atonement."

Sometimes the pastors feel that most of these new songs lack substance, that they're too sugary, too individualistic, and too other-worldly. Sometimes there's an emotional tone to this contemporary worship music that might work well in another kind of church but which just doesn't feel authentic in a traditional or mainline congregation.

Now I would imagine that at least some of you began to glaze over a bit as you attempted to read those last few paragraphs. Or maybe you didn't fully understand some of the terms I just used. If so, don't worry—that's why I wrote this book! If you have no idea what things like "penal substitutionary atonement" or "inclusive language" are about, this book will help you understand what these terms mean and why it's important to your pastors for you to know your way around these issues and concepts a bit as you seek new songs to bring into the worship life of your congregation.

And I promise—I'll do my best to use down-to-earth language that you'll be able to easily understand without a seminary education!

THE AWKWARD CONVERSATION

The last thing most pastors want to do is squelch the enthusiasm of church musicians by telling the band members that the songs they've chosen and spent time on are somehow not "working."

And what's most difficult and awkward for pastors is the whole process of trying to explain to the band members (and the congregation in general for that matter) *why* so many of the popular "contemporary praise and worship" songs are problematic. Many if not most of the musicians who play in church praise bands are not trained theologians, and most of them (us) did not attend seminary. There's absolutely nothing wrong with that. I personally am a seminary graduate and an ordained minister and former pastor, but I'm assuming and hoping that many of you reading this book are church musicians who do not have formal theological training. You are the ones I have in mind most as I write this.

Chances are you are bright, intelligent, talented, and spiritually engaged Christians—not to mention good looking (hey, as long as I'm flattering you I may as well go all out!). But in all likelihood you probably feel a bit lost when it comes to understanding some of the theological jargon pastors tend to use when they're trying to explain why they struggle with the lyrics of many of the praise and worship songs.

And, some of you musicians probably aren't paying that much attention to the words of the worship songs anyway. That just may not be your thing. Or perhaps you find yourselves thinking, "Hey—thousands of people are singing this stuff in churches all the time—what can possibly be wrong with these songs if they're being used as extensively as they are? Why can't our pastor just chill out and not be so anal about every word we say or sing in worship?"

But the simple truth is that words matter.

Language matters.

Theology matters.

The songs we sing in worship matter.

And if you've got a pastor who cares deeply enough about the lyrics of the songs you sing in worship to insist that they have integrity and that they reflect the best of your tradition and your own congregation's understanding of the Gospel, then you are profoundly blessed.

Try to understand the difficult position in which pastors often find themselves. As I already stated, they don't want to throw a wet blanket on anyone's enthusiasm, and they certainly don't enjoy hurting anyone's feelings. They also don't want to seem overly nitpicky and rigid, and pastors are busy people—they may not have the time or energy or desire to go through every piece of music before worship each week to sort out problematic language or ideas in the songs. Most of them would like to be able to entrust this kind of oversight to their ministers of music. I did say "most"—I'm well aware of the control issues and battles that often take place over just who has the authority to choose the songs used in worship. We'll return to that later as well.

It probably also goes without saying that we musicians don't enjoy having to subject our song selections to some kind of "church word police" either.

So the first reason I'm writing this book is because I want to help out with this awkward conversation I've just described. I hope this book is something that pastors can simply hand to musicians in church worship bands, and to anyone in the congregation who cares, and say, "here—let's read this together and talk about it. I think it will help us deepen our understanding of what we need to be doing together in and through the songs we sing in worship."

A NEW GENRE OF CHRISTIAN MUSIC

The second reason why I'm writing this book is because I think it's time for a whole new genre of "contemporary Christian worship music" to come into being. I want to let folks know that there's a new kind of worship music—"Progressive Christian Worship Music"—that is now available.

This book will provide some criteria—the "6 marks"—by which we can determine whether or not a song fits this new genre and why. The 6 marks are meant to be a guide—not a litmus test—and my hope is that they will help us shift the focus of conversation from complaining about what we *don't like* about "contemporary praise and worship music" to what kind of new worship music *we are longing to find* or perhaps even create ourselves and bring into our churches at this point in history.

I am also hoping that this book will stimulate lots of ongoing discussion, interaction, collaboration, co-writing, cooperative publishing, networking, and blogging.

My goals and dreams in this regard are unapologetically bold. I want to help start a movement.

Or probably more accurately, I want to help galvanize a movement that's already begun, and I want to invite you and your congregation to be a part of it. Welcome!

SECTION ONE

The 6 Marks of Progressive Christian Worship Music

CHAPTER 1

Mark 1—An Emphasis on Praise, Justice, and the Fullness of Human Experience

Most of us are familiar with what is often referred to as "praise and worship music." This is the name of the genre of contemporary worship music that you'll find most often on the web or in Christian bookstores. There's some great stuff available in and through these stores and websites and the Christian Music industry they represent. Most of it is about giving thanks, praise, and adoration to God. There's nothing wrong with that, and this book is not going to be a put down or critique of that kind of worship music or the industry from which it emerges (not that some critique might not be warranted!).

But the main point of this first mark is that there's more to worship than praising God.

Praising God is extremely important. It's crucial. Proponents of Progressive Christian Worship Music will also release and promote new songs which help us to praise God.

But there are two primary reasons why many more progressive Christians are a bit weary of some of the "praising" that permeates "praise and worship" music.

First, the praising is sometimes full of what many have come to regard as worn-out Christian buzzwords and clichés. More about this will be explored in chapter six which focuses on the need for "Fresh Language, Ideas, and Images." There are some wonderful worship artists in the praise and worship world these days who are writing fresh and beautiful new praise songs, so I don't want to be unfair or uncharitable here. And, this book is in no way meant to be a put-down of contemporary praise and worship music. There are plenty of Chris Tomlin and Matt Redman songs for example that I think are great, though I usually find myself wanting to tweak the lyrics a bit so that they line up with one or more of the other five marks that we'll get to later on in this book.

But the second and probably more important reason why many progressive Christians sometimes grow tired of the emphasis on praise in a lot of "praise and worship music" is that praise is only one aspect of the overall experience of worshipping God. In addition to praising God, there are many other dimensions or modes of Christian experience and living that we would like to be able to sing about when we gather for worship. We don't have to sing about every area of life and faith in every song or even every service—that would be exhausting. But we want to do more than simply praise God when we sing in the context of worship.

There are some worship leaders and theologians who would probably argue that the only legitimate purpose of worship is to praise, thank, adore, and "magnify" God. Such persons often suggest that songs of exhortation and challenge are not appropriate for worship. But most progressive Christian worship musicians would disagree with this. Yes, we believe that praise and gratitude are key components of worship. But we contend that worship also involves listening for and responding to God's Word and God's presence, getting more deeply in touch with our own hearts and lives in relationship to God, responding to the calls to justice and service, and being in community with the others who are gathered for worship.

The Psalms of course are the primary "book of songs" in the Bible. They were often used by the people of Israel in the context of worship, and they encompass many topics in addition to praising God. There are other emotional and experiential tones in the Psalms—there is disappointment and anger and frustration ("How long O Lord!")—there are laments and words of grief and expressions of guilt and confession. There are calls to do justice, to treat workers fairly, and to offer compassion to the poor. There are reflections on the beauty of the earth and the magnificence of the universe. In other words, the full range of human experience in relationship to God and others is present in this book of "worship songs."

So, Progressive Christian Worship Music will include plenty of what are sometimes referred to as "vertical songs"—songs that help individuals and groups of people lift up their voices in heart-felt praise and gratitude to God.

But Progressive Christian Worship Music will also include "horizontal songs"—songs that encourage us to live out our faith with integrity and passion. Songs that help us to express our sadness, pain, joy, and longing. Songs that call us to be in loving relationships with others, and to do the work of justice and peace, and to find strength to be faithful even when responding to God's call is costly and painful.

FROM PRAISE TO TRANSFORMATION

When every contemporary worship song is a happy song of praise to God, the music and the worship often start to feel a bit mono-faceted and sometimes like a bit "too much sugar." And, constantly telling God how great God is—no matter how sincere we might be—can also start to feel a bit too "flat."

To be blunt, God is not a Divine Ego-Maniac who needs to be told how wonderful He or She is all the time.

Yes, God is great, awesome, magnificent, worthy, etc. But according to Scripture, God is sometimes "still and small," vulnerable, apparently weak, and a friend of moral failures. God also tells us in Amos 5:23 that the songs we sing in worship are nothing more than "noise" in God's ears if they do not somehow lead us to build a more just world. So again, Progressive Christian Worship Music will do more than proclaim how "high and lifted up!" God is.

Please don't misunderstand what's being said here. Praising God is both powerful and necessary. When we praise God we are helped to take our eyes off ourselves and to find our own rightful place in the order and balance of the universe. Praise helps lead us into a place of gratitude and love, and that is always a holy and life-giving place. It reminds us that not everything is about human initiative, and that we are much more contingent and dependent and interdependent than we often want to acknowledge. Praise helps us to be humble and grateful. Praise also somehow puts us in a frame of heart, mind, and spirit in which we are more able to cooperate and co-create with God. Psalm 22:3 tells us that "God inhabits the praises of God's people." In other words, God "shows up" in some uniquely powerful ways when people give thanks and praise, and we want to encourage and experience God's presence in every way we can. So let's sing praise and gratitude to God with our whole beings in musical styles that touch our hearts.

But let's *also* sing about the rest of life in relation to God's desires and intention, and about our own broken and beautiful experiences of life in all its fullness. And, let's sing songs that move us (as individuals and as groups of people) to boldly respond to God's invitations to be agents of healing, love, peace, justice, and transformation.

CHAPTER ONE: QUESTIONS FOR DISCUSSION

1. Think about a time of group worship in which you experienced "praising God" in a particularly powerful way. What was powerful about this experience?

2. Do you have any thoughts to share or to add to what this chapter says about why praising God is important?

3. Think about something you've experienced in worship that was particularly meaningful but that did not have anything to do with praising God directly. What are some of the other things we do in worship in addition to giving God praise? Which are most meaningful to you?

4. Can you think of times when a song (with or without words) has helped you to do something other than praise God in the context of worship? Describe what this song was like and how it touched you.

5. Share with each other some of the songs you've either heard or that you actually use in worship that help you to praise God with passion and joy.

CHAPTER 2

Mark 2—Inclusive language

If inclusive language is a completely new topic to you, this chapter may blow your mind a bit. This is a topic that tends to evoke strong reactions in people. For some folks, inclusive language seems "overly nitpicky," especially at first. For others, this whole area of concern is one in which progressive Christians sometimes come across as being rigid and just a bit too "politically correct."

But, as I've written earlier, language matters. It matters a lot.

Being intentional about inclusive language is ultimately a matter of doing our best to make sure that our language is expressive of what we truly do and don't believe and stand for as Christians. It's about practicing and living out the extravagant welcome and love and respect that is at the heart of the Gospel.

Inclusivity is more than just about gender issues. But when it comes to gender, inclusive language is about making sure that both "maleness" and "femaleness" are fully welcome and respected and therefore *included* in the language we use to talk about God, the Christian faith, and life in general.

THE NEED FOR RESPECT AND MERCY

As strongly as I feel about the importance of using inclusive language, I also think it's vital to approach this subject with great respect for the deep feelings connected to just about every side of this conversation. Folks tend to have strong opinions when it comes to gender related issues, especially in connection with the Church[1] and the history of Christianity.

People also tend to have strong feelings attached to the hymns and songs they grew up singing in church. There have been many attempts in recent years to rework the language of some of the beloved old traditional hymns in order to make the words more inclusive, and these attempts have been controversial to say the least. Any conversation about changing the words of familiar and much loved songs is likely to cause some powerful sentiments to surface.

The importance of being sensitive regarding the issue of inclusive language was underscored powerfully to me by Christian educator Tex Sample in an address I heard him give in 2000.[2] Evidently Rev. Sample learned the hard way how crucial it is to honor the feelings and experiences people have in connection with traditional hymns, even when we may not like either the language or the theology of certain songs.

In the address I heard Tex Sample give, he recounted a church gathering during which he had strongly critiqued the theology and language of the well know hymn, "In The Garden." He talked about things like the "privatistic individualism" of "coming to the garden alone" (we'll get into that more in another chapter). He picked apart the use of exclusively male pronouns for God (we'll get to that in a minute). Suffice it to say that Dr. Sample pretty much tore this old hymn apart, and at times made fun of its message and imagery as being overly sentimental and too "sugary."

But after he had finished his address, a woman from the audience approached him. She was obviously deeply upset. Through tears, she explained that she had been through some terribly painful things in her life, and that the words and meaning of "In The Garden" had literally kept her from committing suicide. She talked about how being able to "walk and talk alone in the garden with her Father God" had helped her hang on to life itself when she was tempted to completely give up hope and do something tragically self-destructive. She concluded by saying firmly to Rev. Sample,

"Don't ever talk about 'my hymn' like that again."

I share the above anecdote to underscore the importance of framing this conversation about inclusive language with deep respect for how emotionally powerful this subject can be. I feel very strongly about the importance of inclusive language. I also want to meet and honor you readers wherever you may happen to be at this point in your life and your spiritual journey. We don't have to ultimately agree when it comes to the importance of inclusive language, but the purpose of this chapter is to at least help you to understand what it is and why it's such an important element of Progressive Christian Worship Music.

INCLUSIVE LANGUAGE REGARDING HUMANKIND

Did you notice that I wrote "humankind" in the title of this section instead of "mankind?" That's an example of inclusive language.

Proponents of inclusive language feel strongly that it is important to include and honor both genders in the language we use, and not to simply use male dominated pronouns when we are referring to both men and women.

We do this based on the conviction that God honors and loves men and women equally, and we go out of our way to use this kind of language deliberately because of our awareness that women have historically been devalued in many cultures, including the culture of the Church. The Church has been particularly "male dominated" over the years in the language it has used publically in the context of worship. The Church has also historically been overtly patriarchal and at times "sexist" in the way that it has structured itself organizationally.

Our overall reading of scripture, together with our own human experience, leads progressive Christians to conclude that any form of exclusion, devaluation, or oppression of women, especially in the name of Christianity, is a tragic misreading of Scripture and of God's original design and intention.

It is beyond the scope of this book to try to get into all the controversies connected to gender and gender roles in particular in the Bible. There are scores of wonderful books and articles written about this for those of you who want to explore this further (Google "inclusive language and the Bible" or "feminist theology" and you'll be well on your way). Suffice it to say for our purposes here though that Progressive Christian Worship Music will always show a deliberate attempt to include and honor the value and dignity of women and men equally.

We do not embrace this priority because we are trying to be progressive or "politically correct." We embrace this priority because we are led by the example of Jesus and the overall message of Scripture to do so.

JESUS WAS RADICALLY INCLUSIVE

We sometimes miss how radically inclusive and "pro woman" Jesus was. This is primarily because we often do not know much about the historical context in which Jesus lived.[3]

In first century Palestine, it was considered culturally inappropriate and religiously taboo for a man to have conversation in public with a woman who was not his wife. It was taboo for a man to publically touch a woman who was not his wife. It was considered "ritually unclean" for a man to touch a menstruating woman. And yet, in the healing stories of Jesus, we find him affirming the value and dignity of women in all of these ways.

Jesus constantly crossed the lines that a "good respectable Jewish man" was forbidden to cross in his culture in order to validate the worth and dignity of women—the "daughters of Abraham." Luke 8 makes it very clear also that Jesus was the kind of rare rabbi who welcomed female disciples. These women traveled around openly with Jesus and the twelve. It is probably not fair in some ways to superimpose the term "feminist" upon Jesus, but he was undeniably and radically "pro woman" in every conceivable way.

MOVING BEYOND OUR OWN CULTURAL CONDITIONING

Many of us grew up just assuming that male-dominated terms such as "mankind" really mean "men and women." This is a very common response I hear when I give workshops that cover the topic of inclusive language. I hear this from men and women, and often most strongly from more conservative women. They say things like, "I know that women are included when someone says, 'mankind.' Why do we have to make such a big deal over such a small thing?"

To this I can only respond by saying that once a person truly "wakes up" to all the tragic and sometimes subtle ways in which women have been (and often still are) historically devalued, then the inclusive, welcoming, all embracing love of Christ within us does not give us the option of not noticing or caring when we sense women are being excluded from our language—or from anything else for that matter.

That was a long sentence, but I think it might be worth reading again . . .

In other words, once you "get it" regarding the oppression and subjugation of women throughout history and how this is reflected in our language, you can't "not get it." You start to see and notice it everywhere, and you begin to realize just how much language really does matter.

On a more humorous note, it was in the early 1980's when I first experienced my own waking up to the importance of inclusive language. When I began to try to use this language more deliberately in worship services, I was amazed by the strong reluctance of some people to even discuss this issue respectfully. This was especially true when it came to experimenting with possible changes to some of the male dominated language in traditional worship liturgies (such as the Gloria Patri). I decided to offer a workshop on inclusive language in a church I was serving, and I found a wonderful little series of film strips (yes—this was back in the "film strip" days!) that had been put together to facilitate discussion of the topic.

In one of the filmstrips, a woman was trying to make the case for the importance of using inclusive language, but every time she did she was told, "We all know that 'men' includes both genders and really means 'men and women." After several such encounters, the woman had to use the rest room. So she entered the "men's room," because of course everyone knows that "men really means 'men and women.'" The reaction she got from the men in the men's room showed her that "men" does *not* always mean "men and women!"

IS IT REALLY THAT BIG OF A DEAL?

As I've said, I think we need to be loving and respectful and also extremely patient and gentle with each other as we grapple with things like inclusive language. I feel very strongly that it's important, but I also don't want to beat others over the head with it.

Sometimes when I suggest changing a lyric from an existing and well known song for example to make it more inclusive, I will also invite people who feel strongly about it to use whatever word is most meaningful to them. This is my way of trying to respect people and give them some room to move at their own pace with all of this.

But ultimately I think this issue really comes down to a matter of embracing and living out the love of God as fully as we possibly can. Because of my personal experience of the power and beauty of God's unconditional and inclusive love, I want the worship services in which I'm present (and certainly those which I am helping to lead) to reflect this love for everyone else as fully as possible.

Whether or not one agrees that using inclusive language is important, the undeniable truth is that there are increasing numbers of men and women in our culture who have awakened to this issue and who are deeply committed to fully honoring and respecting women, their humanity, their rights, and their unambiguous inclusion. I believe God is thrilled with this. And, there's no going back at this point. Despite some of the "push back" that occurs in our public discourse from time to time, there will not be a retreat in progressive Christian circles when it comes to respecting women, and there should not be.

As I already stated, once you develop sensitivity to the presence or absence of inclusive language, it's very difficult to just ignore language that is not inclusive. For me, it's a bit like squeaky chalk on a black board to the ears of my spirit when I hear exclusively male pronouns used in worship. If it's like this for me, I can only imagine how difficult this male dominated language is for women who have personally suffered gender exclusion or oppression. Given that this is the case, why would we not go out of our way to use language that expresses as fully as possible our belief that God loves and values men and women equally?

If there is even only one person present in a worship service for whom the lack of inclusive language would be a stumbling block, why would we not then gladly do everything in our power to remove this stumbling block?

WHEN DONE WELL IT'S NOT VERY OBVIOUS

As far as I'm concerned, the best uses of inclusive language are those which are not noticed at all. The point is not to call attention to the fact that our language is inclusive, though there are times when explaining our deliberate use of inclusive language may be an important thing to do. But the real point is making sure that our language is not *exclusive*. When it's done well, most folks don't even realize that the lyrics of Progressive Christian Worship Music are intentionally inclusive. They just are, and no one has to have it somehow shoved in his or her face (there it is again—notice I didn't just write "his face").

Sometimes when folks attempt to use a well known song and change existing lyrics to make them more inclusive, it's impossible not to notice the change. And sometimes the changes we make are not very poetic or musical or smooth, and this can be a problem. Most of us have experienced changes in song lyrics that came across as stiff or "wooden," and which seemed to cause as many problems as they addressed.

I actually have mixed feelings when it comes to changing the lyrics of older songs. I totally understand and affirm the importance of trying to update the language in order to make these hymns more inclusive, and I've made some of these changes myself at times. But with very few exceptions, I also don't have a problem singing most hymns the way they were originally written. This can be a beautiful way of respectfully acknowledging and honoring our connection to the historical contexts, communities, and composers who brought these songs into being.

Maybe a word could be said before singing such a hymn about our understanding that it was written during a time when language and culture were more patriarchal. Folks could be invited to do whatever they need to do with an "exclusive" pronoun in the song when they reach it. Sometimes it seems arrogant or at the very least ungracious for us to refuse to sing a hymn lyric as it was originally penned. If the theology is just horrible, then we probably should rewrite the entire text or stop singing the song altogether.

But if it's a matter of an exclusive pronoun here and there, I want to be gracious and not always have to have my own way with the language. Then again, perhaps I'm able to be a bit more patient with this process because I'm a man (not to mention white and ordained—the power structures of the Church and of Western culture have always been loaded in my favor!).

I totally understand that some folks—especially women who have been working at great personal cost with this issue for decades—are tired of being patient and gracious. I get that, and I don't blame them at all.

When it comes to new songs being written though, obviously I'm a strong proponent of using fresh language that is always inclusive—so much so that it is one of the key marks of Progressive Christian Worship Music. Anyone who ever sings a song of mine or one that is featured in this new genre will be able to count on the fact that the lyrics will be intentionally inclusive.

INCLUSIVE GOD LANGUAGE

Inclusive God language tends to be even more emotionally complex for people to deal with than inclusive human language.

Simply put, what we're talking about here has to do with the gender of God.

Traditionally, most Christians are accustomed to thinking of God as a male being. People who take for granted that God is essentially male usually point to the fact that the Bible itself refers to God as "He." They'll also remind us that Jesus used the very intimate term "Abba" ("Father," "Dad," or even "Daddy") when he prayed to his "Father God."

Well the point of this chapter is not to argue about the gender of God. It is simply to let you know that increasing numbers of people (and I'm obviously one of them) are convinced that God is not essentially or exclusively male or female. Increasing numbers of us believe that the God of the Bible is either *both* male and female, or somehow beyond gender categories as we understand them altogether.

Certainly, given the very patriarchal culture and time during which the biblical books were written, the Bible offers more male images for God than female. But the female images are also in the Scriptures.

Some scholars suggest that the Hebrew "El Shaddai," usually translated as "God Almighty," could also legitimately be translated, "God, The Breasted One.[4]"

Psalm 131:2 offers an image of God as being like a mother with a breastfeeding child.

Jesus used the image of a mother hen gathering her chicks. (Matthew 23:37)

Beyond that, the words translated "Spirit" in both Hebrew and Greek are feminine nouns.

The "Divine Wisdom" referred to in Proverbs is described in feminine terms (see Proverbs 8).

Genesis 1:27 can legitimately be translated as asserting that both male and female human beings were created in the image of God. If females were created in the image of God, then "femaleness" is clearly a part of the "being" of God.

You get the point.

Progressive Christians are not making up this "God as female" stuff. We're just embracing the fact that these feminine images are a beautiful part of the biblical narrative, and we're being intentional about reflecting this aspect of God's being in the language and images we use.

It's Both/And

One thing that we proponents of inclusive language need to be careful of is to not be so deliberate about including the feminine that we wind up excluding the masculine! It's not about refusing for example to use the word "Father" for God altogether, though sometimes in the pendulum swing of things folks will go through a stage at which it's hard to use "Father" at all. This is especially true for people who have had painful relationships with their own human fathers. When this is the case, the word and metaphor of "father" may actually be so loaded with pain and emotional complexity that it prevents a person from experiencing the love of God in intimate and healthy ways at all.

But the point is to let God be as big and broad and wonder-full in Her or His Being as possible!

Being a father is without a doubt one of the most loving and healing and powerful experiences of my life. I've just recently become a grandfather, and that is off-the-charts wonderful as well! Fatherhood is beautiful. I don't want to lose "Father" as a way of understanding the nature of God's love. But when we're using the overall metaphor of Divine Parent as a way of understanding God, I want to include the powerful image of God as Mother as well.

There are also times when it's important to embrace names and images for God that are beyond gender or personification altogether. One of my favorite names for God at present is "Holy One." There is no gender at all in that term. Others may know and experience God as "Source," "Creator," "Beloved," "Healer," "Energy of the Cosmos," etc. These names for God side-step the gender issues completely.

No one name will ever exhaustively convey the fullness of who God is.

And every name is at best just an image or a metaphor—just one way of trying to describe this amazing Being who will always be beyond our ability to fully describe with human language. All the names for God together would not be enough, and any one name is at best only a partial description.

In the end, maybe the healthiest thing we can do is show a good deal of humility when it comes to the limitations of language. Sometimes I think the ancient Hebrews were wisest of all when it comes to talking about God or addressing God directly. Out of respect for the ultimate mystery of the Divine, they forbade themselves to even speak the name (Yahweh) of God at all. They realized that the moment we name or label something (or someone), we begin to reduce the essence of that person or thing. So the Hebrews wouldn't even write or speak the name which God had used when speaking with Moses on Mount Sinai. Instead they used a substitute word, Adonai, which is translated LORD in English.

This was their way of acknowledging that God will always be more than the names and words we use to describe who God is. And yes, as you may have guessed, even the word "LORD" can be complicated!

THE PROBLEM WITH "LORD"

This one will probably sound over the top to some of you, but the simple truth is that increasing numbers of folks are having a hard time using the word "Lord" (or LORD as it's usually rendered in English translations) for God. The problem tends to have two different dimensions.

First, for some, the term "Lord" reminds them of feudal society in which there were "lords and lassies." In that sense then "Lord" is a male term, and all of the same issues that we've been exploring so far come into play regarding gender exclusivity.

For others, "LORD" is problematic because of the "power over" implications of the term. For these folks, this is too domineering of a word to use for God. These people don't see God as one who wants to simply dominate or control humans or to be some kind of Divine puppeteer. Instead, they see God as a being who wants to be in mutually respectful and loving relationship with humans and who wants to *co-create in partnership* with human beings.

Progressive Christians who struggle with using the word "Lord" are reminded also of Jesus' words in Matthew 20:25-28 in which he talks about true greatness in God's eyes. Jesus said, "In the world, human benefactors 'lord it over' others, but it will not be so among you. Instead, the greatest among you will be the servant of all."

So "Lord" is a problematic term for increasing numbers of progressive Christians because we don't experience God or Jesus as one who wants to "lord authority over humans." Jesus made it very clear that he himself came as one who serves rather than dominates (Luke 24:27).

My only problem with this critique of the word "Lord" is that it often fails to acknowledge and honor the tender intimacy and emotional closeness that the name "Lord" carries for so many Christians.

Despite the "power over" implications described above, many Christians use this name for God with the exact opposite connotation emotionally. It's actually a very intimate term of endearment, and it would be a big loss emotionally for them to stop using this name for God. So I can see both sides of this. Again, let's be gracious and flexible. We need to be careful that in the process of not "lording over others," we wind up actually being domineering and unyielding when it comes to our opinions about these things!

I used to use the word "Lord" a lot in my own personal relationship with God, and earlier songs of mine sometimes included this term. It's a beautiful and intimate name for God in my own personal experience. But again, knowing as I do now that this term can be a stumbling block emotionally and spiritually for many others, I find myself searching for different names to use for God in my music, and I rarely use the word "Lord" (or "LORD") when I'm speaking to or about God in the context of public worship.

But I'll be honest—even though I tend to avoid using this name for God for all the reasons I've just articulated, I still catch myself calling God "Lord" in my own personal times of prayer. Again, this term is a tender and beautiful way of speaking to God in my own experience, and even though my head has pretty much let it go, my heart still seems to use it when I'm not "thinking about it." I'm okay with that.

Bottom line—you probably won't see the word "Lord" used much in most of the newer music in the Progressive Christian Worship Music genre. But there may well be some exceptions, and as is the case with many of these issues we're exploring, you'll find a wide degree of opinions about this word among Christians who would enthusiastically refer to themselves as progressive.

There may be songs in this genre that have been around for a while that meet all of the marks of Progressive Christian Worship Music while still using the word "Lord" for God at times. Let's be gracious with each other as we also strive to be deliberate and soulful regarding our use of language.

Concluding Remarks

I hope you've got a good feel now for what inclusive language is about and why it is important enough to be named as a key mark of Progressive Christian Worship Music. One more thing you should know is that it is virtually impossible for a mainline Protestant clergyperson to have gone through seminary in the past forty years or so without having been deeply exposed to the importance of inclusive language.

As already stated, once one's eyes and ears and heart are opened to this issue, it is impossible not to notice language that is exclusive in terms of gender. So this may be why your pastor seems particularly concerned with all of this. She or he was most likely trained to make sure that the language of public worship is inclusive for all the reasons we've explored in this chapter. It's not an easy thing for pastors to be trained to use inclusive language in seminary and then to have to deal with the fact that many local congregations are still either resistant to or completely unaware of the importance of inclusive language. I hope you will become an advocate for inclusivity in all of its forms in your worshipping community.

Of course some clergy disagreed and pushed back against inclusive language when in seminary and beyond. If you or others in your music ministry are opposed in some way to the ideas at the heart of inclusive language, here's hoping that you can at least have a good conversation with each other regarding this topic, and that you'll pray for the Spirit's leading as you consider the ideas we've explored in this chapter.

Chapter Two: Questions For Discussion

1. You may not need any written questions in order to have a lively discussion about the content of this chapter. Did anything strike you in such a way that you really want and need to discuss it with your group? If so, just name those things and go for it!

2. Is this the first time you've been asked to think about "inclusive language?" Is this a subject that is already important to you? Does this topic make you uncomfortable? Defensive? Why do you think this issue is often so difficult for congregations to discuss?

3. How do you feel about changing lyrics to older hymns and already published songs in order to make them more inclusive?

4. Bryan wrote, "Ultimately I think this issue really comes down to a matter of embracing and living out the love of God as fully as we possibly can." What do you think about this statement?

5. Reflect together on Bryan's statement, "As far as I'm concerned, the best uses of inclusive language are those which are not noticed at all."

6. Why do you think that the gender of God is a topic that carries so much energy for a lot of people? What's at stake that makes this difficult to discuss sometimes? What is needed in order to work constructively with this topic?

7. Do the contemporary praise and worship songs you sing reflect an awareness of inclusive language? If not, what do you think about changing words here and there in order to make these songs more inclusive? By the way, it is not a violation of copyright laws to make slight changes in a lyric, and I encourage you to change any of my lyrics if that helps your congregation to worship God with more integrity and joy.

8. Bryan wrote, "In the end maybe the healthiest thing we can do is show a good deal of humility when it comes to the limitations of langrage." Respond a bit to this statement.

CHAPTER 3

Mark 3—Progressive Theology

This third mark is definitely the most difficult of the 6 marks to explain. In fact, this chapter was initially over twenty pages long! I quickly realized that I was trying to cover way too much ground. Part of the reason for this initial overreach was due to the fact that we are touching upon some theological issues in this third mark that can be complex and extremely controversial. It felt irresponsible on my part to open up these topics without going into some serious depth.

I also wanted to give you a sense of where I stand at this point regarding some of these theological questions so that those of you who have followed my ministry and who care about me will know how to best pray for me! I'm kidding, at least in part, but the truth is that I have a hunch that the ideas expressed in this chapter are going to be confusing and disturbing for some readers. Out of love and respect for you, and out of my own desire to be as clear as possible regarding my own positions, I wanted to give these topics the extra time and space that they deserve.

So what I decided to do after considerable thought was to briefly state what a number of these potentially complex issues are here in this chapter, and then to include more substance in the final section of this book for those of you who really *want* to explore some of this theology and where I'm coming from personally in more detail.

What Is Emphasized Theologically In Progressive Christian Worship Music

Progressive Christians tend to be deeply drawn to the welcoming, inclusive, unconditional love that is at the heart of the biblical message. A phrase that's often used in progressive Christian circles is "extravagant welcome." This welcoming love leads progressive Christians to place a premium on honoring and respecting the spiritual journeys of all persons, wherever they happen to be in their lives.

At our best, progressive Christians encourage all people—including people who embrace other religions or no religion at all—to understand that we are all loved and accepted by God. So, Progressive Christian Worship Music will help proclaim the good news that God's love for all people is "radically inclusive," merciful beyond our wildest dreams, and unconditional.

The lyrics of the songs we sing will be inclusive both in terms of "inclusive language" and also in terms of their focus on a God whose boundless grace and love is extended to all persons regardless of their doctrinal beliefs, race, tribe, ethnicity, sexual orientation, or even their religion.

In other words, the focus is on the divine love which constantly expands the circle of Spirit-centered fellowship in order to include others. There is no "we and they" in a circle. This inclusive love will cause us to cross and erase lines that separate people or that cause people to feel inferior, unclean, unworthy, or unacceptable.

More About Grace Than Law

Another succinct way to put this is to say that Progressive Christian Worship Music will be more about grace than law. Sometimes progressive Christians are accused of focusing so much on things like grace and mercy and forgiveness and love that we don't seem to emphasize the requirements of the law very much at all. By "law," I'm referring to things like the 10 Commandments and all of the precepts and ordinances and holiness codes that are found in the Bible.

All that can be said at this point is that there is at least *some* truth to this accusation! But please don't misunderstand me. Progressive Christians do not casually dismiss or disregard biblical laws or standards. Neither do we side-step the truth that there are often extremely costly and tragic consequences when individuals, communities, or nations fail to embrace the ways of God. But, we will always emphasize God's grace and love more than any notion of judgment or punishment.

We do this not because we are "bleeding heart liberals," or because we "don't stand for anything." We do this because Jesus constantly chose mercy over law, and we're trying to follow him! This was Jesus' whole point in verses such as Matthew 9:13 in which he said, "Go and learn what this means, 'I desire mercy, not sacrifice.'"

Grace that has the final word over law is a huge part of what we stand for—because this is what Jesus stood for. Again, this doesn't negate the laws in Scripture. We're well aware of Jesus' statement that "not one jot or iota of the law will pass away." (Matt. 5:18). It's just that when there is a choice between strict and rigid adherence to a religious rule and showing mercy and love, Jesus always chose to emphasize mercy and love. Progressive Christian Worship Music will reflect this way of understanding both Jesus and the heart of God.

It is interesting that the only people Jesus ever seemed to truly clash with were the Scripture quoting religious authorities (Pharisees and scribes, etc.) who were too sure that they knew how to rightly interpret God's laws. They tended to be overly confident that they knew who was and was not acceptable to God or "right with God" and why. They looked at the sinners, moral failures, and outcasts among Jesus' closest friends and followers and accused Jesus of being "too welcoming."

Jesus was often accused by good Scripture quoting religious folks of "breaking the law" because he insisted on offering mercy, healing, and full acceptance to people who were considered to be sinful or unclean according to biblical standards. Instead of judging and rejecting them as "sinners," Jesus affirmed their value and worth as children of God, extended grace and forgiveness, invited them into his community of faith, stood with them when others were critical or unjust to them, and *then* on some occasions also told them to stop doing anything they knew was wrong ("go and sin no more" John 8:11).

Even though he was criticized for being too open and welcoming, Jesus stood up to critical religious authority figures who were more focused on obeying religious rules than on showing love and grace and mercy.

Unfortunately, it didn't take very long after Jesus was killed for his scandalous "extravagant welcome" to be tempered and toned down once again by Church authorities. It's almost as though we humans just can't handle the freedom of love into which Jesus invites us. We so often seem to prefer lists of religious do's and don'ts to a more open-ended invitation and mandate to love ourselves and others as Jesus did.

Not long after Jesus' death his followers began to start new systems of "in and out," or to somehow cling once again to the old ones. But God kept breaking through to open up and expand the circle of grace. Remember Peter's rooftop vision in Acts 10:9-15, for example, and also Paul's call to invite the non-Jewish world (Gentiles) into the family of God.

Again and again in Scripture God challenged people to move beyond seeing the essence of the spiritual life primarily as a matter of obeying or living up to a moral, ethical, or behavioral code. Ultimately, the biblical vision is about *responding to how loved and accepted we already are*—not about "measuring up" to some standard so that God *will* hopefully consider us acceptable.

Progressive Christian Worship Music will constantly remind us that while Jesus did not negate the importance of the commandments and precepts of the Hebrew Scriptures, the only "law" he ultimately insisted upon was the law of Love. According to Jesus, loving God and loving our neighbors as we ourselves would like to be loved is ultimately what matters most (along with honoring the gift of Creation, which the overall biblical narrative also calls us to do).

What Is Not Emphasized In Progressive Christian Worship Music

There are certain theological emphases that you will not hear or see much in Progressive Christian Worship Music. Explaining these theological positions is where this chapter could get way too long! So again, there is an additional chapter in the third section of this book called "More About Progressive Theology" for those of you who want to explore some of these concepts further. Here is just a brief list of some of what is deliberately *not* a focus of Progressive Christian Worship Music.

1. **Penal Substitutionary Atonement (PSA):** Progressive Christian Worship Music is sensitive to the increasingly widespread conversation going on in the Church these days (and in progressive Church circles in particular) regarding the doctrine of penal substitutionary atonement. This doctrine is being seriously questioned and in many cases rejected altogether by many progressive Christians.

   For our purposes here, this means that there will not be much talk in our lyrics about Jesus *having* to be sacrificed on the cross in order to pay the price for the sins of others. Even more specifically, there will not be a focus in our music on Jesus having to take a Divinely willed *punishment* (which is what the word "penal" stands for) that God would have insisted we sinful humans receive if Jesus were not punished in our place. Jesus' death on the cross may well be mentioned in our music, but the focus will not be on Jesus being punished in order to satisfy the requirements of God's holiness and perfection.

   Progressive Christians tend to feel that the doctrine of PSA winds up painting a picture of the heart and character of God that is overly judgmental, legalistic, vindictive, unloving, and even abusive. Many progressive Christians tend to suggest that this doctrine and related ideas were later developments of the Church rather than part of God's or Jesus' own intentions.

   We realize that this is where progressive Christianity can come across as confusing and offensive and even heretical to Christians for whom these ways of understanding the cross are part of the very core of the Gospel message. So please read the additional chapter on progressive theology in the third section of this book if you'd like to try to understand this more deeply, or get a better sense of where I am personally on these issues.

Please also understand that there is no one way in which progressive Christians will approach topics as nuanced, complex, and controversial as PSA. Some of us have found ways to embrace this doctrine (or portions of it) by redefining it to some extent. Others reject it altogether.

What is most important for you to know is that this is a "hot topic" these days, and increasing numbers of progressive Christians and pastors no longer believe that penal substitutionary atonement—Jesus being punished by God so that we do not have to be—is a necessary or healthy way of understanding why Jesus went to the cross. This is one of the most recurring problems that many more progressive pastors have with a lot of "praise and worship" music, because Jesus dying on the cross to pay the price for our sins tends to be a key focus in many of the songs that come out of that industry.

2. **"Blood Sacrifice Theology":** Progressive Christians who struggle with the doctrine of PSA also tend to struggle with doctrines regarding blood sacrifice and the blood of Jesus for most of the same reasons. So you will not find many references to things like the "cleansing blood of Jesus," or being "washed in the blood of the Lamb" in Progressive Christian Worship Music.

    Again, there will be a range of positions on this topic, but most progressive Christians do not believe that God *required* the blood of God's son Jesus in order to pay the price for the transgressions of others. More is written about this in the final section of this book for those of you who want or need to get into this more deeply.

3. **Escaping From This World:** Instead of leaving or escaping from this broken world or waiting for Jesus to come again to "take his people home" while this world reaches some tragic and cataclysmic end, progressive Christians focus on being individuals and communities

God can use in order to *engage with* this world and help make it more loving and just. Instead of condemning the world or judging it, Progressive Christian Worship Music will include a strong emphasis on social justice—bringing this world and its systems and structures more into line with God's vision of love, compassion, and wholeness.

In other words, rather than focusing on getting to heaven after we die, Progressive Christian Worship Music will focus primarily on the quality of life here on earth. You might say that our focus is on trying to make life on earth, as much as possible, a reflection of heaven. This should not sound too unusual, utopic, or radical. After all, this emphasis is built right into the prayer of Jesus (the "Lord's Prayer") that we pray almost every week in every church—" . . . Thy will be done *on earth as it is in heaven.*"

It is not that progressive Christians reject the hope and "blessed assurance" that life continues beyond the grave in the realm we usually refer to as heaven. There are probably some progressive Christians who no longer focus on life after the death of the body at all, but there are many of us who very much affirm the beauty of the hope of the "life to come," or "the next realm," or "another dimension," or whatever phrase one might want to use for the mystery of what lies on the other side of the human bodily experience.

The point for our purposes here is that Progressive Christian Worship Music will not focus primarily on "getting to heaven." Instead the focus will be on having loving, Spirit-centered relationships with God and with others, and on working for justice and peace (the biblical vision of "Shalom") here on earth. In other words, we will focus more on the *transformation* of this world, than on *"being saved"* from it.

4. **Being Saved From Hell:** We do not believe in what many have referred to as "the Gospel of fire insurance"—that the primary reason to believe in Christ is to avoid the literal fires of hell. It's not that we ignore the reality of "hell." Jesus mentioned hell in several of his teachings, and most progressive Christians take these teachings very seriously. We just tend to interpret the meaning of these teachings differently.

It's way beyond the scope of this chapter or this book to get into the subject of hell in much detail or depth, but for a brilliant, succinct, and easy to understand example of how I would personally deal with this topic, check out the chapter called "Hell" in Rob Bell's book, Love Wins.[1] This will give you a beautiful example in my opinion of how one can take the reality of "hell" very seriously without regarding it as a literal place of everlasting torture people go to if they don't "believe in Jesus" in a particular way.

Another way of putting this is to say that there will not be a big focus in Progressive Christian Worship Music on what theologians have traditionally referred to as *justification*. Instead of justification—what it takes for us to be "justified" before God or to "be right with God" so that we can avoid the punishment of eternity in hell, we focus on the fact that God already loves and accepts us all—just as we are. This does not mean that God is pleased with all of our choices or how we are living our lives, or that serious changes might not need to be made if we want to live fully in rhythm with God's will and intentions. Neither does this mean that sin does not exist and need to be dealt with.

But progressive Christians tend to agree with ideas like this one which was expressed in a sermon by Rev. Nadia Bolz-Weber;

> . . . *in the end, we aren't really punished for our sins nearly as much as we are punished by our sins.*[2]

In other words, it's not that God is waiting, like an angry parent, to give us an everlasting spanking when we finally "get home." We do not believe that God is *mad* at us and waiting to punish us if we don't "get saved." And we don't see God as a strict, moralistic or legalistic Judge who is compelled by "Divine justice" to punish those who violate God's standards of perfection.

Instead, any punishment we ever receive as a result of our sin comes in the form of the painful things we and others bring into our own lives and this world when our choices are not in line with the ways of God. And make no mistake about it—these painful things can be absolutely devastating and horrific beyond description for us, others in our lives, for the entire human race, and for the earth itself. "Hell" is all too real in this regard. Again, read Rob Bell's chapter on hell for a more thorough explanation of what I'm describing here.

We do not take sin—"missing the mark"—lightly, and neither does God. I can't remember where I heard this, but someone once said, "God loves us just as we are, but God loves us too much to leave us just as we are!" Progressive Christians affirm the never-ending process and hard work of trying to live our way into the challenges of Scripture and especially the teachings of Jesus. But most of us would affirm that all people, simply by virtue of being God's children, are loved and accepted and fully received by God (both here on earth and in the life to come).

Again, there will be a wide range of opinions and positions and theologies among progressive Christians regarding the specifics of how we understand God's amazing grace and acceptance and how we hold this unconditional love in tension with some form of accountability to God and others for how we live our lives.

5. **Jesus being the "only way" to God:** This is really just one more expression of the "extravagant welcome" and inclusivity that is at the heart of progressive Christianity. To be very straightforward, there will be no references in Progressive Christian Worship Music to Jesus being the only way to God, or about Christianity being the only "true faith."

We don't ignore verses such as the often quoted John 14:6, in which Jesus is quoted to have said, "I am the way, the truth, and the life. No one comes to the Father but by me." But as with the subject of "hell," progressive Christians tend to have different ways of interpreting what Jesus was saying in this verse. Again, it's beyond our purposes to tackle this in depth in this book, but a great example of some wonderful progressive insights on this text can be found in Dr. Eric Elnes' compelling book, The Phoenix Affirmations.[3]

Progressive Christians would not contend that all religions are the same, or that there is nothing unique about the Judeo-Christian vision. But we do joyfully and unapologetically affirm Truth wherever it is found, including in other religions. We do not believe that being a Christian means that we need to close ourselves off to the presence of Truth in other spiritual visions or that we must somehow put down other religions in order to follow Jesus.

CHAPTER 3: QUESTIONS FOR DISCUSSION

1. Bryan mentioned that there is a tension in the Bible between grace and law. How do you work with this tension yourself? Why do you think some people tend to focus more on law, and some more on grace? Do you agree that Jesus, when forced to somehow choose, chose love, grace, and mercy over religious rules? Is it possible to be "too welcoming?" How do you hold God's unconditional love in tension with being somehow accountable to God for how we live our lives?

2. Do you feel clear that you understand what the "doctrine of penal substitutionary atonement" is? If not, discuss it a bit and help each other get clear about this.

3. What was your initial reaction to reading that many progressive Christians reject the doctrine of penal substitutionary atonement? Were you offended? Concerned? Relieved to know that others are questioning this way of understanding Jesus' death on the cross? How about the same questions regarding blood sacrifice?

4. What do you think about the Nadia Bolz-Weber quote, ". . . in the end, we aren't really punished *for* our sins nearly as much as we are punished *by* our sins?"

5. What do you think and/or believe about hell? Do you think it is legitimate to interpret biblical teachings about hell in ways other than hell as a literal place or condition of eternal punishment and agony?

6. What do you think about other religions? How did Bryan's remarks about respecting Truth wherever it's found, including in spiritual visions other than Christianity, strike you?

CHAPTER 4

Mark 4—An Emphasis On Both The Individual And The Community

After that last chapter on "Progressive Theology," you'll probably be relieved to know that this chapter is much less heavy and not very controversial!

Simply put, Progressive Christian Worship Music will include songs that hopefully touch and move our individual hearts and that help us to have intimate experiences of God's presence in worship. But in addition to giving us opportunities to worship God as individuals, Progressive Christian Worship Music will also call us beyond ourselves into fellowship with others, into loving and healthy relationships, and into groups of people who are working together to transform the world.

There is absolutely nothing wrong with songs that encourage individual believers to nurture personal and intimate relationships with God. We need them. In fact, my experience over the years has led me to believe that many people in mainline congregations are longing to be able to "feel their faith" more personally and also to have experiences of worship that will move them individually.

But we also need songs that remind us that the Christian journey is a call into a *community* of believers.

Many pastors in more progressive churches are weary of the individualism that is characteristic of so much contemporary "praise and worship" music. In other words, one of the most common critiques pastors in mainline churches offer regarding praise and worship music is that it's just too "me centered."

Brian McClaren, an author and well known leader and mentor in the Emerging Church movement, wrote a wonderful article called "An Open Letter to Worship Songwriters." As Brian writes on his website (www. brianmcclaren.net), this letter . . .

. . . *originally was published in Worship Leader Magazine, but its life continued online and it has been translated into a number of languages since then. In it, I expressed a number of frustrations that I felt regarding the music commonly used in our churches. In particular, I complained about the hyper-individualism and even spiritual narcissism in so much of our "worship music." At times, as a friend of mine put it, we seem to be congratulating God for making us feel so good and meeting our personal wants and needs so nicely.*

In McClaren's "Open Letter to Worship Songwriters," he writes,

Too many of our lyrics are embarrassingly personalistic, about Jesus and me . . . . listen next time you're singing in worship. Most church goers NEVER reflect on the lyrics. If they did they would never sing them. THINK about what you are singing. If you don't agree with the lyric then don't sing it.

It's about how Jesus forgives me, embraces me, makes me feel his presence, strengthens me, forgives me, holds me close, touches me, revives me, etc., etc. Now this is all fine. But if an extraterrestrial outsider from Mars were to observe us, I think he would say either a). that these people are all mildly dysfunctional and need a lot of hug therapy (which is ironic, because they are among the most affluent in the world, having been blessed in every way more than any group in history), or b). that they don't give a rip about the rest of the world, that their religion/spirituality makes them as selfish as any nonChristian, but just in spiritual things rather than material ones.

Brian gets right to the heart of what I'm trying to say in this chapter. There is a tendency in a lot of "praise and worship" music to make it sound as if God exists to serve *me!* I sometimes call this the "God as personal Jeanie motif." It's not that it's wrong to sing about our individual relationships with God, or to be grateful for what "God has done for me."

But the healing and wholeness we receive from God as individuals is meant to free us up to become more available to others, to take our eyes off ourselves, and to find the piece of God's dream for the world (i.e. mission) that is ours to help carry. Yes, God loves, heals, and sets us free as individuals. It's wonderful to sing about that. But we need to sing about more than what God has done for individual persons, and we need to make sure that there is more to our worship and our theology than a focus on individual persons loving and being loved by God.

THERE ARE NO 'PRIVATE' CHRISTIANS

Progressive Christians believe passionately that the Christian faith is also about entering into a community of believers, believing and working together to make this world more loving and just, and about becoming a member of the "Body of Christ"—the Church. Christianity is not just about helping individual persons believe in God. It's not just about helping individuals live happy lives on earth and then get to heaven when then die.

When I lead retreats for teenagers (and for adults as well), there's a statement I often ask in the course of a game of sorts that I like to play. The game or exercise is called "Here I Stand," and I would imagine some of you have experienced it in one form or another. Here's how it works.

Everyone is gathered in a room. The leader then makes a definitive statement, and the people gathered are then asked to show "where they stand" with regard to the statement. One wall in the room is designated as the place where the participants will stand if they *agree* 100% with the statement. The opposite wall is designated as the place where they will stand if they *disagree* 100% with the statement. If they agree, but not too strongly or with some reservations, then they will stand somewhere between an imaginary line in the middle of the room and the wall that represents total agreement. You get the idea.

After everyone stands where they choose to in response to the statement, then the leader invites anyone who would like to speak to say a few words about why they are standing in their particular spot. No one is ever forced to say anything, and no one is forced take a stand on a question he or she would rather not answer publically. If participants would rather not answer then they just stand in the middle of the room. We then spend a little time talking about the statement. There are no arguments permitted, and one of the key ground rules is that all opinions expressed will be honored and respected. It's a great exercise to use to invite a group to explore a difficult question or issue, and I encourage you to steal it and use it if you like.

One of the statements I love to make when using this exercise is, "You don't have to be a part of a church to be a faithful, biblically based Christian."

Almost always, just about everyone in the room (except for the pastors and perhaps a few others) will stand near the wall of complete agreement.

Teenagers are often playfully trying to climb the wall!

When asked to explain their position, people often say things like, "I feel closer to God in the beauty of nature than in a church building," or "You don't have to go to church to believe in God." When they say these things, I usually agree with them. We don't need to go to a church building in order to believe in God. We don't need to be Christians at all in order to believe in God and feel close to God. I often feel closer to God in nature than in church buildings myself!

A big part of the value of this exercise is creating an atmosphere in which it feels safe for people to risk sharing what they really think and believe, even if the opinions expressed differ greatly from my own or from what the leaders of the group would like to hear. So I never aggressively disagree or try to somehow trump someone's honest opinion or position.

But eventually, either I or someone else makes the point that as far as biblical teaching goes, there is really no such thing as a "private Christian." Jesus called his disciples to be a part of a community. The idea that spirituality is just a private thing that people somehow "do" as isolated individuals apart from others is not a biblically based idea (apart perhaps from a true calling into deep solitude for the sake of the world, such as that of a hermit, which I won't explore at this point).

No, we don't necessarily need other people in order to believe in God, or maybe even to feel close to God personally, but to be a Christian is to be a follower of Jesus, and Jesus was about creating a people—not just a bunch of individual believers.

When Jesus taught his disciples to pray, he did not instruct them to begin by saying, "*My* Father in Heaven." He said, "*Our* Father." He didn't say, "Give *me* this day *my* daily bread." He said, "Give *us* this day *our* daily bread."

It's not that Jesus didn't also have a very personal relationship with God. He obviously did. He often withdrew from the crowds and spent all night in prayer alone with God. But in many ways his whole ministry was about gathering a *group* of people who would embrace his teachings and establish a *people* who would continue the work he was sent to do.

And, it's worth noting that Jesus' group involved people who did not always get along with each other, and who may not even have liked each other or chosen to hang out with each other if they had not been called into the group by Jesus and by the Spirit of God. It wasn't about "finding my people." It was about responding to Jesus' invitation to follow the way of Christ *together*—even when it's hard and you don't all get along, and even when you don't naturally feel like loving each other, let alone like "washing each other's feet." There's a big difference.

Again, there's nothing necessarily *wrong* with "Jesus and me" (or "Christ and me" or "God and me") songs. But we also need songs in which the whole community is addressing God collectively and singing to God together as one body, and we need songs that remind us that we need each other to truly follow in the way of Jesus—songs that help deepen our sense that we can be and do so much more together as groups of people than we can as isolated individuals.

So there will be a deliberate focus on moving from "I and me" to "us and we" in Progressive Christian Worship Music. This doesn't mean that every song has to do this. But more often than not, Progressive Christian Worship Music will *both* help individual believers worship, *and* remind us that we are members of a worshipping community.

To give just a quick example of how this might work in a song, one of my choruses that gets used a good deal in churches these days is called, "To Be Loved This Way." It is often used as an "assurance of pardon" after a prayer of confession. There are two verses. The first one is personal and focuses on the individual. The second verse moves into the collective and focuses on the community. Here are the lyrics;

If it's true you love me as I am
And not as I think I should be
Then I'm free to face the parts of me
I'm tempted to deny
God you know all my laughter and all of my tears
You know where I've been and you know why I'm here
And you know it heals my deepest wounds to be loved this way

If it's true you love us as we are
And not as we think we should be
There we're free to trust the Mystery
And love beyond all fear
God you know all our laughter and all of our tears
You know where we've been and you know why we're here
And you know it heals our deepest wounds to be loved this way [1]

MOVING FROM THE PERSONAL TO THE POLITICAL

In one of the many workshops on Progressive Christian Worship Music which I've helped to lead, we were discussing this fourth mark about moving beyond individualism. One participant added that he felt that Progressive Christian Worship Music should also emphasize a movement from "the personal to the political." He pointed out that "political" doesn't mean "partisan politics." It's more a matter of focusing on things that affect the common good—life in the "polis." His point was that so much contemporary worship music emphasizes the personal feelings and experience of the individual, and that we also need songs that emphasize the role of Christian love and action in the public realm.

This movement from the personal to the political was certainly alluded to in the chapter on mark one—Praise, Justice, and The Full Range of Human Experience—but it is a point well taken and worth mentioning here as well. Progressive Christian Worship Music will deliberately call us beyond being preoccupied with our own personal wellbeing and into loving action and advocacy with others on behalf of our local towns and institutions, our wider communities, our states, nations, the entire human family, the earth, and all of creation.

Again, there's no need to do this with in every song or in every liturgical moment, but the overall thrust of Progressive Christian Worship Music will always involve a call to focus both on the personal *and* on the collective.

Chapter 4: Questions For Discussion

1. What did you think about Brian McClaren's suggestion that the words of so many praise and worship songs are too "privatistic?" He wrote, *"At times, as a friend of mine put it, we seem to be congratulating God for making us feel so good and meeting our personal wants and needs so nicely."*

2. Why is focusing on the biblical call into community so important? What is missing when we reduce Christianity to a matter of isolated individuals being close to God?

3. Many folks in mainline churches actually complain that their worship services and Christian experience are not personally moving enough, and that this is why many people leave mainline churches and go to churches that focus more on a "personal relationship" with God. Have you found this to be the case? How can we do a better job of both nurturing individual relationship with God and also embracing the call into Christian community?

4. What do comments like, "I went to church and I didn't get anything out of it so I stopped going" have to do with the focus of this chapter?

5. Do you agree that "there are no private Christians?" Does this mean that we need to go around talking about our faith in public all the time?

CHAPTER 5

Mark 5—Emotional Authenticity

I was speaking with a United Church of Christ clergy colleague named Gregg Brekke about Progressive Christian Worship Music and about this book, and he shared something with me that takes us right to the heart of what this chapter is about. Rev. Brekke told me that he used to pastor a congregation that was trying to bring some more contemporary music into its worship services, and that the three "rules" he gave his music leaders when it came to the message, language, and theology of new worship songs were the following;

1. No "bloody Jesus."
2. No "Rambo Jesus."
3. No "boyfriend Jesus."

The "bloody Jesus" issue (blood sacrifice theology) was covered a bit in chapter three, and is further explored in the final section of this book. The "Rambo Jesus," the muscular "triumphal Jesus," is a macho Christ usually depicted as wanting to "kick the Devil's butt" or "take something back for God." This will also be dealt with in the chapter called "More About Progressive Theology."

But "boyfriend Jesus" has everything to do with what this chapter is about.

When music is written or chosen for congregational worship, composers and those who choose songs for worship are literally putting words into other people's mouths that we hope they will be able to sing and mean with integrity. For this to happen, the lyrics need to feel emotionally real to the congregation.

One of the reasons why certain contemporary praise and worship songs sometimes don't feel quite right in many mainline churches is because these songs tend to come out of a church worship culture that is much more demonstratively emotional and extroverted than that of most traditional churches. There tends to be an almost romantic tone to many praise and worship songs in these more emotionally expressive congregations. Jesus and God are often sung to in a way that a lover would sing to a boyfriend or girlfriend.

While this may work well in certain fellowships, the simple truth is that many if not most people in mainline churches have never thought about or related to God in this more intimate, romantic way. So it often feels strange to folks in mainline churches to start singing things like, "My Jesus, I love you," or "I keep falling in love with you over and over again," or "You're everything to me." By the way—notice the individualism? "*I* love you." "*I* keep falling in love . . ." ". . . everything to *me*."

It's not that very intimate relationship with God is wrong or inappropriate. Quite the contrary. There have been Christian disciples (many of whom we would probably refer to as "mystics") since the Church's earliest centuries who have had intensely intimate experiences with God as "the Beloved." And of course there is the Song of Songs in the Bible itself. Much of the imagery in that book is downright erotic! We don't want to lose this tradition of intimate and emotionally rich ways of understanding the human/Divine relationship. For those of us for whom this way of knowing God is indeed a part of our experience, there is no need to in any way put this down or consider it somehow inappropriate.

But it's fair and accurate to say that not many people in mainline or progressive Christian circles tend to easily embrace romantic language and metaphors when it comes to their relationships with God. For some people in more traditional churches, using romantic language is an embarrassing and "overly familiar" way to talk to or about God. For others it can wind up somehow feeling trite, disrespectful, irreverent, or just plain theologically and emotionally "off."

Blogger and ELCA Lutheran pastor Nadia Bolz-Weber captured what I'm pointing to here in her own wonderful style on one of her blog entries;

> *Lutherans aren't really known for using "personal relationship with God" language, and I cringe at Evangelical-Speak—like calling Jesus your "Personal Lord and Savior"—it can so often feel like Western Individualism run amuck in religion. As though in your contact list Jesus is listed between your Personal Chef and your Personal Trainer. A friend of mine describes this idea of Jesus as "your bearded girlfriend who wants to be your life coach." All this is to say that using "personal" to describe how I relate to God can feel problematic to me, mainly because it borders a bit closely on religious narcissism. And I, perhaps unfairly, associate this language of personal Lord and Savior with emotionalism and a smug affect of sanctity and I'm suspicious of the whole thing and would prefer to just talk about theology.*[1]

Sometimes the discomfort folks in traditional churches feel with this more emotional way of addressing God or Jesus or the Spirit has very little to do with theology or the nature of their relationship with God at all. Many people in mainline churches come from ethnic backgrounds, families, communities, and church cultures that did not encourage them to be very emotional about *anything*, let alone their faith! Both by temperament and by the emotional environment in which they were raised, they tend to be more reserved.

This doesn't mean that they are not deeply committed to God or that they are not passionate in their own way about their faith. They may simply be much more predisposed to worship quietly, to want and need times of silence in worship, and to prefer music and lyrics that are less overtly emotional. We need to be sensitive to this and to respect this as we attempt to bring new styles of music into our worship services.

REGARDING EMOTION WITH SUSPICION

For complex reasons, the role of emotion in worship is at best a tricky thing in most traditional churches. Many pastors in mainline churches were taught in seminary to regard emotion in the context of worship with a degree of suspicion. They are quick to point out that being close to God is not just a "warm fuzzy feeling." They will point out, and rightly so in my opinion, that feelings come and go, and that God is still present and active in our lives even when we don't *feel* God's presence in some emotional way.

Many pastors also rightly point out that worship should not be reduced to what some will call "emotionalism" (a faith and worship experience that is primarily about feeling hyped up emotions), and they don't think worship should be a matter of coming to church just to get a "God buzz." There's nothing wrong with hoping that vital worship will help us to get "charged up" spiritually. In fact I would contend that vital worship *should* help renew our strength in Christ and help us to find courage and a sense of being "lifted up." But needing an emotional high of some kind in order to *feel* spiritually alive can be almost like a drug, and one can get a good "Jesus high" in this way and yet avoid the biblical mandates to do justice, love people we may not like or want to hang out with, speak Truth to power, and do the hard work of being the people of God. There are times when a Christian life will involve commitments that may not always "feel good."

Pastors in more progressive churches are also very aware that people can be manipulated by emotional appeals, and they are often cautious regarding the role that music can play in this emotional manipulation. So there are some thin lines that we need to be aware of here, and we need to learn how to maintain a sense of balance when it comes to music and emotion.

On the one hand, of course we musicians want to use the power of music to help create an atmosphere in which people's hearts are touched and moved by the Presence and Spirit of God. Let's be unapologetic about that. We *want* people to feel moved by the songs we use to help facilitate dynamic and meaningful worship.

But we also need to be very careful that we don't try to somehow *manufacture* a "feeling of God's Presence" by using music and words that we know will produce a certain emotional effect. So understand that some pastors are probably going to get a bit uneasy when the music used in worship is evoking deep emotional reactions in people—unless it is done with great respect, awareness, maturity, and integrity. As with most things, the emotional power of music can be used positively and it can be used negatively. It can evoke profound emotional responses that help people sense the presence of God, and it can be used to manipulate people.

Ultimately, this is one of the reasons why worship leaders and musicians need to do our own internal work so that we can use the emotional power of music and lyrics in ways that are respectful and honorable and truly worshipful. We don't want to blindside people emotionally, or somehow *make* people feel things that aren't authentic for them, or use music to create an emotional atmosphere in which people may feel pushed or even embarrassed into responses that they were not truly ready to offer.

Thin lines all over the place here. In the end, it's about our being as sensitive as we possibly can to the leading of God's Spirit as we minister in and through our music.

THE HEAD AND THE HEART

Another thing to be aware of is that fact that mainline, traditional, or progressive Churches have a tendency to be at least a bit more intellectually oriented than many evangelical or fundamentalist churches. Please don't hear this as a suggestion that more conservative Christians are less intellectually astute than progressive Christians. That is certainly not true and it would be wrong, arrogant, and unfair to assert this.

But in general, my experience has been that mainline and progressive clergy and church members tend to be a bit more "in our heads" when it comes to our faith and our services of worship. We tend to value hard-nosed biblical scholarship (as defined by our more liberal-leaning theological seminaries and traditions), and we tend to be much more comfortable talking *about* God than talking *to* God. Similarly, we tend to be more comfortable *thinking about God* than with trying to *experience* or *feel* God's presence.

This is not a critique. It's an observation.

The human mind with all of its amazing capacity is a precious gift from God and we glorify God by using our intellects rigorously. But one thing that's happening a great deal in progressive Church circles is that folks are longing for an expression of Christianity that involves both deep thinking *and* deep feeling.

As many people have recognized more recently, large numbers of mainline and progressive Christians never really learned how to talk about our faith at all. Even when we've had powerful experiences of God's presence in worship or in other contexts, it's almost as if we were never given a vocabulary with which to discuss it. Not that these experiences always need to be discussed, but the point is that most of us in mainline church circles were never taught how to *feel our faith* or how to discuss God's movement in our lives in ways that seem authentic and real.

Many people are hungry to grow in this regard and to learn how to talk about and live an experience of faith that has intellectual integrity as well as emotional depth and power. It seems as though there is a fresh longing and openness in more progressive circles for a faith "with both a head and a heart." I am convinced that Progressive Christian Worship Music will play a key role regarding a meaningful response to this longing.

One of the reasons why a large portion of mainline pastors don't care for many of the "praise choruses" that come out of the more evangelical praise and worship industry is that these short repetitive choruses often seem theologically trite. There is not enough theological or intellectual meat in many of these songs for a lot of pastors. These choruses would be examples of songs that may evoke a lot of feeling, but which don't have much substance connected to them.

To put it another way, there is "too much heart (often in the form of sentimentalism) and not enough head" in many of these worship songs. In the next chapter, we'll take a look at what it means to try to stay in the "deep water" of both heart and mind rather than in the "shallows" of too much emotion without enough theological content—or the other way around.

The Creator obviously blessed human beings with both intellectual and emotional capacities. We are always both. That's how we were created, and the two are meant to go together. The first commandment actually is a mandate for us to love God with all of our *mind, heart, and strength.* It's right there—love God with our minds *and* our hearts. So, once again, what we need in Progressive Christian Worship Music are songs that involve theological depth and intellectual vigor as well as emotional power and the ability to touch and move our hearts. These things are meant to go together.

BEYOND ANTHROPOMORPHISM

There's one more thing I'd like to point out in this chapter on emotional authenticity. There are increasing numbers of progressive Christians who for many reasons find themselves drawn to what theologians often refer to as "process theology." To greatly oversimplify what process theology is about, it often includes experiencing God as a "Loving Energy" or "Source" or some other metaphor that is not overtly "personal" at all.

The theological term often used for our tendency to relate to God in "personal" ways is "anthropomorphism." Yeah, I know—big word. You don't need to remember it!

But anthropomorphism refers to the human tendency to think of God in "human terms." No problem with that. We're humans after all. It's meaningful for many of us to try to understand God with images and metaphors and concepts that are human-like and that therefore seem accessible to our hearts and minds.

But we also need to be careful not to project our own shadows and shortcomings onto God, or to somehow reduce the vast mystery of the Divine by making God as small and limited and even as petty as we humans can sometimes be. As philosopher Blaise Pascal once put it, "God created humans in God's image, and humans returned the compliment."[2] The character of the God who is preached and proclaimed and written about is often just as vengeful, resentful, and biased as we humans can be at our worst.

To be sure, one of the primary biblical ways of understanding the Being of God is to think of God as a Divine Parent (Father or Mother). There are countless other "personal" images for God or the Spirit in Scripture as well. But many people in more progressive churches find it as least *as* meaningful and maybe even more so to try to think of and experience God in terms and images and metaphors that are not "human-like" at all.

For these persons, the romantic language of much current praise and worship music is even more of a problem than it is for others. In fact it's often a total turn off to them. So let's just be aware of this and do our best to write and share some new worship music that these folks I'm describing can "feel" and sing authentically as well. We can't please everyone all the time, but let's try to create some songs that folks who are less anthropomorphic in their faith can also enjoy.

Just to give you an idea of what lyrics like that might look like, here are the words to a new chorus of mine that I've been using a lot lately. The song is called "Fully Alive."

> *I want to open my heart a little wider*
> *Let Spirit in a little deeper*
> *Love with a Love that's on fire*
> *And be fully alive!*

Nothing complicated about these words. I just avoided personal pronouns and references to God as a "Being." And, by the way, the verses of this song use plural pronouns ("we" and "us")!

CHAPTER 5: QUESTIONS FOR DISCUSSION

1. What was/is your reaction to the "boyfriend Jesus" remarks in this chapter? Is there a romantic dimension to your relationship with God or Jesus?

2. Is there a difference between relating to God "romantically" and relating to God "intimately?"

3. Have you experienced some form of contemporary praise and worship music that either made you uncomfortable emotionally or that did not feel "authentic" to you?

4. Why do you think some people are more comfortable with emotional expression than others? Is there a "right" or "wrong" way to be in this regard?

5. Do you agree that worship in mainline or traditional congregations tends to be more head-oriented than heart-oriented? If so, why do you think things are this way?

6. Do you agree that there is a need for worship and music that has both intellectual substance and the ability to move people's hearts? Have you ever experienced a time of worship in general or a piece of worship music that had both intellectual substance and the ability to move people's hearts? If so, describe this a bit if you can—what made it both intellectually substantive and emotionally moving?

7. Do you tend to think of God "anthropomorphically?" What is either lost or gained by imagining the Divine in less "personal" ways?

CHAPTER 6

Mark 6—Fresh Images, Ideas, and Language

The main point of this sixth mark is that we want to avoid worn out Christian clichés and buzzwords in Progressive Christian Worship Music. We also want to use fresh language and ideas in order to "tell the old old story" in ways that will connect as meaningfully as possible with people living at this point in history.

It's not that the words, "Praise the Lord" are somehow wrong or off-limits, although I've already shared with you the problem that increasing numbers of progressive Christians have with the word "Lord" in the chapter on inclusive language. The emphasis here though is on trying to be creative and fresh. We want Progressive Christian Worship Music to include songs that use images and metaphors for God that open our hearts and imaginations in new ways.

Richard Bruxvoort-Colligan is a wonderful progressive Christian songwriter and liturgical musician whose music often illustrates this sixth mark regarding fresh images, ideas, and language. One of my favorite songs of his is called "Ground And Source Of All That Is."[1] The lyrics speak for themselves . . .

Ground And Source Of All That Is

By Richard Bruxvoort-Colligan

Ground and source of all that is
One that anchors all our roots
Being of all ways and forms
Deepest home and final truth

We live and move in you

Lover of ten thousand names
Holy presence all have known
Beauty ever welcoming
Mystery to stir the soul

We live and move in you

Nature by whose laws we live
Author of our dna
All-compelling call to life
Drawing one and all the same

We live and move in you

Energy of heav'nly spheres
Spark within the insect mind
Unseen pulse to charge our plans
Bringing order and surprise

We live and move in you

Call to kindness, call to serve
Freedom for our chosen course
Guide and friend for all who dream
Nourished by our ground and source

We live and move in you
© 2004 This Here Music/Worldmaking.net (ASCAP)

There's nothing radical or controversial in terms of the messages in this song, and yet there is nothing clicheish or "heard that before" in these words either. The music is as beautiful and singable as the lyrics. I highly recommend that you check out Richard's website and explore other songs of his as well.

THE IMPORTANCE OF IMAGES

It was no accident that Jesus' primary teaching methodology involved the use of stories (parables), metaphors, and questions. And just about every good communicator knows that while facts and information can be important, it is stories and images that "get to people" in ways that open hearts and lead to transformation.

As James Smith states in his book, <u>Desiring the Kingdom</u>;

> *It's not so much that we're intellectually convinced and then must muster the willpower to pursue what we ought; rather, at a precognitive level, we are attracted to a vision of the good life that has been painted for us in stories and myths, images and icons. It is not primarily our minds that are captivated but rather our imaginations that are captured, and when our imagination is hooked, we're hooked (and sometimes our imaginations can be hooked by very different visions than what we're feeding into our minds) . . . Thus we become certain types of people; we begin to emulate, mimic, and mirror the particular vision that we desire. Attracted by it and moved toward it, we begin to live into this vision of the good life and start to look like citizens who inhabit the world that we picture as the good life. We become little microcosms of that envisioned world as we try to embody it in the here and now.*[2]

Songs that communicate loving and life-giving content using fresh images and ideas are powerful teaching tools in the hands of the Holy Spirit. They stay with us long after the music has ended, and continue to "work on us" psychologically and spiritually as they take root in our imaginations.

Looking Again At Things Like "Royal" Language

There are no ideas or images that are somehow essentially "wrong" from the perspective of Progressive Christian Worship Music. But it may be that some of the metaphors we've used for centuries in church circles and in church music are no longer communicating as effectively as they once did. Some folks in more progressive churches for example are questioning the use of "royal language"—referring to God as "King" or to Jesus as "Prince," etc.

This is tricky stuff, because this language is obviously all over Scripture, and some of the most popular praise and worship songs still use it. Again, there is no need to be rigid or legalistic about any of this, but the simple truth is that most modern nations don't have kings anymore.

For someone who hasn't grown up in church, even a concept such as the "Kingdom of God" can be increasingly difficult to find meaningful or compelling. Many folks are now wondering if there might be additional ways of referring to God's Kingdom that will somehow get through to a modern listener (or postmodern or gen X,Y, millennial, etc.) more effectively than royal images.

Some progressive Christian songwriters suggest using phrases like "God's Dream," or "God's Realm," or God's "Kindom," for example. This is probably why my song, "Dream God's Dream" is one of the most widely used songs in my catalogue at this point. A term like "God's Dream" avoids the dominant male or patriarchal implications of Kings and Princes (remember the mark of inclusive language), and also the hierarchical (power over) implications of Kingdoms (once again, please read the chapter in the second section called "More About Progressive Theology" to more fully grasp what I'm alluding to here).

Which Issue Should Be on the "Front Burner?"

Sometimes it's hard to balance all of these theological issues and concerns and to try to decide what's most important. For example, there is a singer/

songwriter whose music and ministry I like a lot named Derek Webb. He has a great song called, "A King and a Kingdom" in which he prophetically challenges some of the idolatry inherent in the ways certain Christians, particularly more right-wing conservative Christians, combine biblical faith with patriotism. This is the kind of theme—naming and exploring the dangers of overly nationalistic Christianity—with which many progressive Christians would deeply resonate. Here are the lyrics of the chorus of the song;

My first allegiance is not to a flag, a country, or a man
My first allegiance is not to democracy or blood
It's to a king & a kingdom [3]

So you see, Derek uses "royal imagery"—which I've just suggested may not be very fresh—to articulate his very important critique of dangerously nationalistic or patriotic Christianity. And the song works. It makes its point and communicates powerfully. This is why I wouldn't want to say, Progressive Christian Worship Music will *never include* the use of royal imagery. We need to let this whole thing breathe more than that!

Once again, we need to be humble and open enough to love older language when and where it helps us to best express what we're longing to say in our own context. At the same time, we need to also push ourselves to search for creative new ways to sing to and about God and the life of faith.

REPETITION AND THE IMPORTANCE OF SUBSTANCE AND DEPTH

One of the most common critiques I hear of praise and worship music, especially "praise choruses," is that the lyrics tend to be too repetitive, overly simplistic, and shallow.

I don't think that repetition in and of itself is *necessarily* a problem.

Many people who don't care for "praise choruses" have no trouble at all with the music of the *Taize* community in France, for example. Taize chants are repeated again and again in an almost trance-like fashion so that the worshipper has a chance to truly hear and feel and absorb the meaning of the lyric in a deeply spiritual way. Countless people have found these songs and liturgies to be profoundly powerful. Repetition can work. Sometimes repetition of a simple phrase or text is the very thing needed to give the lyric and melody an opportunity to penetrate into the depths of our beings. Some folks love praise choruses precisely because they can be easily learned, memorized, and then truly "sung from the heart" without having to read lyrics or musical notation.

Christopher Grundy, a singer/songwriter, ordained UCC minister, and professor of Preaching and Worship at Eden Theological Seminary, said something in an address I heard him offer that provides a key to whether or not the repetition of a lyric "works."[4]

Drawing from the insights of Gabe Huck, a Roman Catholic pastoral liturgical theologian, Dr. Grundy said,

> *If we are going to ask our congregation to repeat a lyric again and again, then we need to make sure that the lyric itself can 'bear the weight of repetition.'*

I love that.

And then citing Lenora Tubbs Tisdale in her book Making Room At The Table,[5] Christopher suggested that,

> *The lyrics of a chorus need to be deep enough to 'avoid the shallows.'*

Dr. Grundy shared Tisdale's insight that there are "channel markers" we learn to recognize and which warn us when we are in danger of venturing off into "shallow waters" lyrically and theologically. These shallows can exist on the "heart side" of things—too many touchy feely songs with sweet words but little depth of content—and they can exist on the "ritualistic/intellectual" side of things—too many dry boring songs that have some content but very little emotional power or spiritual depth.

The challenge, Christopher Grundy contended, is to stay in the middle of these two shallow extremes. As he poetically suggested,

That's where the deep water is found.

So if we're going to use choruses, we need to ask ourselves, "are these words worth taking the time and energy to sing over and over again? Do they bear the weight of repetition? Are they deep enough to avoid the shallows?"

ONE OF MY FAVORITE CHRISTOPHER GRUNDY SONGS

In my opinion, Christopher Grundy is one of the more gifted writers of choruses in the Church these days. He is uniquely skilled at writing lyrics that are brief, simple, yet substantive, and putting them to music that is immediately accessible and easy to pick up without being overly simplistic or trite. This is no small accomplishment, and I highly recommend his music. One of my favorite choruses of his that exemplifies his gift for simplicity with depth is his song, *"Here In This Place;"* (Copyright 2002; Hand and Soil Music; all rights reserved).[6]

Holy One may your presence here open our minds
May your Spirit among us help us to find
We are rising up now like a fountain of Grace
From the Holy Ground here in this place

Are you beginning to recognize some of the "marks of Progressive Christian Worship Music" in this song?

Holy One—a fresh, not overly used name for God, and inclusive in terms of gender.
. . . *open our minds*—not just "my mind," but *ours*

May your presence here open our minds—not just about praising God, but about opening us up as well.

We are rising up now like a fountain of Grace—what a beautiful, fresh, image and idea.

Nothing clicheish at all in this song. Christopher wrote it initially for an annual conference meeting of the Iowa Conference of the UCC. Many of Iowa's churches include farmers and farm families. So a song about the sacredness of "place" and "Holy Ground" spoke with particular power and depth to the heart language and mindset of this worshipping community.

The need for substance and depth is not just something that applies to choruses. One of the reasons why many clergy in mainline churches prefer traditional hymns to contemporary praise and worship music is because they regard the newer songs to have less content. Sometimes this is because of the brevity of a chorus, but sometimes the songs just seem shallow compared to the theologically rich hymns that have had staying power for generations in the Church.

So in addition to choruses with depth that are worth repeating, we need new verse/chorus songs with substantive theology and language that reflects the best of who we are as Christians at this point in history.

I call these "contemporary hymns."

As I mentioned earlier, one of my most widely used worship songs is "Dream God's Dream." This is a good example of a contemporary hymn, and I'll close this chapter by sharing the lyrics of this composition, and then by very briefly pointing out how this text embodies the 6 marks of Progressive Christian Worship Music.

By the way, this piece was originally written as a theme song for the first annual "Winter Weekend" senior-high retreat for the Southern Illinois Conference of the UCC in 1991. This yearly retreat is still going strong, and it takes place each January during Martin Luther King, Jr. holiday weekend. You can catch some of Dr. King's "I Have a Dream" speech reflected in the text.

Dream God's Dream

By Bryan Sirchio
Copyright 1991; Crosswind Music

Dream God's Dream
Holy Spirit, help us dream
Of a world where there is justice
And where everyone is free
To build and grow and love
And to simply have enough
The world will change
When we dream God's dream

I'm dreaming of a world, where the color of one's skin
Will mean less than what's within the person's heart
A world where water's clean, and where air is safe to breathe
And every child born has enough to eat

Chorus

I'm dreaming of the call God is offering to me
How to use my energy and my best gifts
To do the work of Christ—to say God, please use my life
To spread your healing Love and to live your Truth

Chorus

I'm dreaming of the way that I want my life to go
I've got hopes and I've got goals I'd like to meet
I'm reaching for the stars, but I won't forget the scars
Of Christ who died to show that the Dream's for all

Chorus

A QUICK LOOK AT "DREAM GOD'S DREAM" IN LIGHT OF EACH OF THE 6 MARKS;

1. **Mark 1: (Praise, Justice, and the fullness of Human Experience)** This song is both a prayer to God at points (thus has a vertical praise-oriented aspect to it), and it's also about God's vision of justice and peace and wholeness for the world (a more horizontal life-changing and world-changing aspect).

2. **Mark 2: (Inclusive language)** There are no gender dominant pronouns or images for God in the song.

3. **Mark 3: (Progressive Theology)** On the positive side, note the focus on the welcome to all, the vision of justice for all, and also on the transformation of this world rather than escape from it. In terms of what is *not* emphasized, there is no penal substitutionary atonement and no blood sacrifice theology even though the cross is alluded to in the third verse.

4. **Mark 4: (The Individual and the Community)** The chorus of the song contains plural pronouns (us and we), and the verses are sung from an individual perspective (I and me). Both are present, with the focus involving a movement from the personal to the public.

5. **Mark 5: (Emotional Authenticity)** Especially when sung, this text can take people to very intimate places with God as they reflect on how to live out God's call upon their lives and use their gifts for ministry. But there is nothing in this text that would embarrass someone emotionally.

6. **Mark 6: (Fresh Images, Ideas, and Language)** "God's Dream" is a new term being used more and more instead of "God's Kingdom." The ideas of justice for all, food for hungry children, a clean and healthy environment, discovering gift and call, and being reminded that Christ's call can be costly, are all themes that will easily take us into "deep water" biblically, theologically, personally, and as congregations. These themes are relevant, challenging, and worthy of repetition.

CHAPTER 6: QUESTIONS FOR DISCUSSION

1. Bryan wrote, ". . . we need to be humble and open enough to love older language when and where it helps us to best express what we're longing to say. At the same time, we need to also push ourselves to search for creative news ways to sing to and about God and the life of faith." Are there older and familiar phrases or images that are particularly meaningful to you even though they are sometimes critiqued now because of their "outdated" language? How can we best honor these in light of everything you've read in this book so far? Are there new phrases, images, and ideas that have opened up something fresh and new to you? Share some of these with each other.

2. Bryan wrote, "So if we're going to use choruses, we need to ask ourselves, 'are these words worth taking the time and energy to sing over and over again? Do they bear the weight of repetition? Are they deep enough to avoid the shallows?'" Think about some of the brief choruses you may be using in worship or with which you are familiar. What is an example of one which may *not* bear the weight of repetition? What is an example of a chorus or newer song which *does* bear the weight of repetition?

3. What are some of the ways in which we sometimes "run into the shallows" in worship? Where is the water deepest for you in worship? Where is the deepest water for you in the worship service you most often attend? Is music connected to this?

4. Be silent for a moment, and see if you can come up with a fresh "name" for God that has meaning for you. Interesting things sometimes happen when we allow ourselves to play a bit with language. I have a song for example that is about an encounter I had with a little girl who was a street orphan in Haiti. I was thinking about Jesus' words in Matt. 25 in which he said, "I was hungry and you fed me." I call this girl, "Little girl Christ" in the song, and that has become an image of God for me. You get the idea. If you're willing, share some of these with each other. Have some fun with this . . .

SECTION TWO

Worship, Songs, and Ego Work

CHAPTER 7

Worship And The Purpose of Worship Music

Now that we've taken a good look at the 6 Marks of Progressive Christian Worship Music, I'd like to open things up a bit and share some thoughts about worship itself and what it is we are hoping our "worship music" will help us to experience and accomplish.

WHAT IS WORSHIP?

So what is worship anyway? Why do we worship? What is the role of music and group singing in worship?

All kinds of books and articles and resources have emerged in response to these huge question. Chances are I'll just be reminding you of some things you already know, but I think there's value in doing that as we try to deepen our sense of how to worship God in and through music.

First, worship, among other things, is not just something we do or experience in a church building for a certain amount of time. It can be that of course, but it's more than that. It's a way of being. A way of living. Worship is a total life response to God's love for us. It's about doing our best to live every moment of every day in such a way that God is honored and respected and loved. In this broader sense, I and many others would contend that worship is a lifestyle. As Amos 5:23 reminds us, our "worship music" is little more than noise in God's ears if it is not rooted in lives of justice and kindness and Spirit-centered action.

Sometimes though, we set aside specific portions of time and energy in order to deliberately focus our awareness and attention on the presence, beauty, and will of God. We might say that worship in this sense is a matter of intentionally expressing heart-felt love, appreciation, and gratitude to God for the gift of life and for the joy of knowing and experiencing God's "Being." There are no objectively right or wrong ways to do this, and true worship is more about the intentions of the heart than any techniques or rituals or actions—or songs!

Yet actions and rituals and songs usually *are* involved in expressing the worship that flows from our hearts. We use silence, all of our senses, words, symbols, Scripture, and art (including music) in the process of worshipping.

So what's going on in these experiences of worship?

In his book, The Hour That Changes Everything, South African pastor, musician, and author John van de Laar responds to this question regarding the purpose of worship by sharing a penetrating quote from Rev. William Temple. William Temple was a priest in the Anglican Church in Britain and was the Archbishop of Canterbury from 1942 until his death in 1944. According to Rev. Temple;

> *To worship is to quicken the conscience by the holiness of God, to feed the mind with the truth of God, to purge the imagination by the beauty of God, to open the heart to the love of God, to devote the will to the purpose of God.*[1]

Rev. van de Laar uses the five statements contained within this quote as the framework of his book, and I recommend The Hour That Changes Everything to those of you who would like to reflect even more deeply on the purpose of worship.

Rev. Temple's quote reminds us that while God is certainly "worthy to be praised," one of the reasons why worshipping God is so important is because of the impact that vital worship has on the individuals and communities who are offering the worship. Worship changes *us.* When we experience worship that is alive and true, we place ourselves in a position to be spiritually shaped, formed, renewed, and over time—transformed by God.

Again from van de Laar's book;

> *What we do on Sunday is intended for one purpose, and one purpose only—to bring human beings into deep, passionate, life-changing encounters with the God who made us and to whom we long to return. For Marcus Borg worship "is about creating a sense of the sacred, a thin place". A thin place is a term used in Celtic Christianity to refer to moments, activities and places where the visible world of our daily lives and the reality of God's presence intersect. A thin place is a place in which we become aware of the reality of God within and beyond our physical world, and in which we are opened up to encounter with this divine reality. In expanding this idea, Borg continues: The diverse forms of Christian worship do this in different ways. At one end of the spectrum, the enthusiasm of Pentecostal worship can become a thin place by mediating an almost palpable sense of the presence of the Spirit. At the other end of the spectrum, Quaker silence serves the same purpose. In liturgical and sacramental forms of worship, the use of sacred words and rituals creates a sense of another world.*[2]

Our times of worship often help us to regain our spiritual focus and to "come back home" to God if and when we have somehow wandered from God's intentions for our lives. Worship helps us to find our bearings again and to re-ground our beings in the One who matters most and in the relationships and aspects of life that matter most.

Worship also helps us to look beyond ourselves—beyond the private agendas and schemes that so easily become self-serving and other-harming—so that we can reconnect our lives with God's love for everyone and everything. In other words, worship helps remind us that life is not all about *us*. It helps us to find ourselves once again inside of God's greater Story, instead of trying to somehow make God fit within the confines of *our* smaller stories.

This greater Story is revealed to Christians, among other things, through the witness of the Bible.[3] So worship will involve hearing and responding to biblical texts. Biblically grounded worship helps reset our point of reference so that the God of Scripture is once again rightly at the Center of everything—including our own personal lives—and so that we can step into our "larger selves" or our "true selves" *in God* once again.

Worship also helps us to find release from our insecurities and fears. God knows how much pain and suffering is brought into our lives and this world because of fear. Worshipping God somehow helps to melt away our fear and anxiety so that we can find the courage and strength we need to trust God with our lives and to realize once again that God is our ultimate source of security. I sometimes think of worship as "the antidote to fear." Worship helps to reestablish and build up our ability to place our trust in God. That's where the peace is—in truly trusting God—or as pastor Gordon Cosby puts it—"in putting all our weight down on God."[4]

When it comes to finding comfort and healing in times of great sadness and heavy burdens, heart-felt worship lifts our spirits and opens our beings to the very Source of healing and hope. We're reminded in worship that God is with us, that God feels the things we feel, and that God will walk with us and even carry us when our hearts are broken and our strength is gone. We are reminded that God has always been faithful and present in times of trouble, and that God will eventually bring us into times of gratitude and gladness once again.

Worship also provides us with opportunities to respond again and again to God's love for us. We are reminded that the best way we can live out our gratitude to God is by offering ourselves—all we are and all we have—back to God, and by committing ourselves (or recommitting ourselves) to living lives of loving service to others. Worship helps us renew our commitment to working with other people, in the power of the Spirit, to make God's Dream of justice and peace for the world and all of creation a present reality.

TO RECAP THE POINTS JUST MADE

So what is the purpose of worship music? Quite simply, it is to help us experience and do all the things I just suggested that worship is about (and any you may think of that I left out!). Our worship music should help us to worship!

Here's a brief list of all the points just made in a way that might be a bit easier for you to work with.

Worship is About . . .

1. Deliberately focusing our awareness and attention on the presence and beauty of God; intentionally expressing heart-felt love, appreciation, and gratitude to God for the gift of life and for the joy of knowing and experiencing God's "Being;" creating "thin places" in which worshippers encounter God in life-changing and transforming ways.

2. Regaining our spiritual focus and "coming back home" to God if and when we've somehow wandered away. It's about finding our bearings again and re-grounding our beings in the One who matters most and in the relationships and aspects of life that matter most.

3. Helping us to look beyond ourselves—getting beyond the private agendas and schemes that so easily become self-serving and other-harming—moving beyond our small stories and stepping back into God's larger Story as revealed to us through Scripture.

4. Helping us to find release from our insecurities and fears; putting our trust in God and finding our true security in God.

5. Finding comfort and healing in times of great sadness and heavy burdens.

6. Responding again and again to God's love for us. Opening our very beings to the transforming presence of God. Being reminded that the best way we can live out our gratitude to God is by offering ourselves—all we are and all we have—back to God, and by committing ourselves (or recommitting ourselves) to living lives of loving service to others.

7. Helping us renew our commitment to working with other people in community. Being empowered by the Holy Spirit to make God's

Dream of justice and peace for the world and all of creation a present reality.

As I suggested at the outset of this chapter, I probably haven't written anything here that you didn't already know about worship. And perhaps I've left out something significant. But I hope I've offered you a renewed sense of how profoundly powerful and consequential worship can be. As John van de Laar's book title suggests, real worship (as opposed to simply going through the motions in some boring and detached way) can play a key role in how God "changes everything."

I hope this excites you and that you realize how important your musical leadership is! And I hope you have a fresh sense of the crucial role you play in your congregation's worship life as one who helps provide the music that greatly impacts the depth and quality of the worship that will happen in your congregation.

The music you choose to help your congregation worship passionately will be used by God to change and perhaps even save lives. It will help people find and be found by God. It will greatly impact the overall identity and mission of your congregation, and hopefully even help to change the world. This is important stuff!

CATCHING A WAVE OF GOD'S PRESENCE

My good friend and wonderful singer/songwriter Andra Moran[5] recently shared a brief article with me that was written by Matt Redman. Matt is an English praise and worship singer/songwriter and one of the leading figures in the praise and worship music industry. He is the composer of the well known praise song, "Heart of Worship," and a highly sought after worship leader for large conferences and events in many evangelical church circles. Matt alludes to something in his article that I'd like to explore a bit. His article was titled, "The Constant Expectation of the Heavenly."[6]

The title of the article gets right to the point. In more evangelical church cultures, there is a hope and even an expectation that when people start singing and praying and offering heart-felt praise to God the Holy Spirit may well "show up" in ways that are surprising, tangible, and deeply powerful. There is a hope that the Spirit will somehow "take over" the worship service, and perhaps lead the congregation into a spontaneous experience of God's presence that could not possibly have been planned ahead of time. Matt wrote the article from which I'm excerpting just two days after experiencing one of these powerful times of God's Spirit "breaking through" at a worship conference;

On the second night of the gathering, as we worshipped our hearts out through music, something happened. It was an "otherly" moment—a heightened sense of the glory and grace of God. As we journeyed deeper through spontaneous singing and prayer, there was a very real sense of adventuring in the Holy Spirit before the throne of God. For me it was one of those meetings you dream for as a worship leader—and once you have such an encounter, there's no going back. It's a little like surfing a great wave and then waiting for the next big wave to come. You're hesitant to leave the water until you encounter more of the same. In a sense, all you can do is wait in expectancy, knowing there is nothing you can do to conjure up that moment—but you determine to make yourself ready to flow with the next big wave that arrives.

So every time we get up to lead worship, we must do so with a longing for heavenly and holy moments. And a knowledge that no amount of striving or experience could ever make these moments happen. They cannot be manufactured or formularized. They are grace, pure grace. The only thing we can do is prepare our hearts, and create an environment of dependence. As Oswald Chambers said:

"Complete weakness and dependence will always be the occasion for the Spirit of God to manifest God's power".

Perhaps the key to holding onto a constant expectation of the heavenly is to remember that worship is a spiritual thing. Sometimes we get caught in the mindset of merely seeing our congregational times together as a 'musical thing'. We see and hear instruments, we pour out our voice through song. Many have settled simply for these elements of our congregational gatherings—and pleasant and uplifting as these things may be, they are only the mere shallows of the mighty deep. In the most powerful and profound worship meetings, "deep calls to deep." It is a spiritual event—the deep places in us responding to and resonating with the deep places of God. As 1 Corinthians tells us, the Spirit searches all things, even the deep things of God. Our prayer should become, "Holy Spirit of God, you are the ultimate worship leader. Lead us today into the depths of God". This prayer and posture is a worship leading essential—the constant expectation of the heavenly.

I have made the point several times in this book so far that worship is more than an experience of "good spiritual feelings." It's not just about getting our weekly "Jesus high." But I can't help but wonder sometimes if the worship culture and liturgical traditions of mainline denominations haven't somehow factored out the possibility, let alone the *expectation*, that God's Spirit might actually "inhabit our praises" and take us into some mystical and transforming experience of the "deep things of God" that can't possibly be controlled or "pulled off" on our own. Would we even want such a thing to happen in our congregations?

If it were truly God's Spirit and not some "stylistic vibe" we were trying to manufacture on our own in order to convince ourselves that our worship is unique and powerful, I would welcome this kind of breaking through by the Holy Spirit. It would probably not be right or authentic for every kind of congregation, and we would need to discuss this "possibility" with the congregation and play around a bit with our liturgical forms in order to create space in our worship for something like this to happen in a way that feels real to us.

But my point is that there is something wild and unpredictable about being thoroughly open to God "doing a new thing" in our worship that I would like to see more progressive congregations welcome. If it's about being fully open to being led by God in worship, let's be as wide open as we possibly can be!

And, while there is comfort and a certain kind of depth in the familiarity and repetitive nature of many of our liturgies and "orders of service," perhaps many folks who are bored with some of our traditional ways of worship would find this possibility of God's spontaneous breaking through to be exciting and alive. Then again, they might be freaked out and run if such a thing ever happened!

But in all seriousness, I sometimes wonder if this kind of worship rarely if ever happens in our more mainline and progressive congregations primarily because we are not open to *allowing* it to happen. We like to try to be in control of things such as time—God forbid worship should go longer than our allotted sixty minutes! Or perhaps we fear what kind of weird or back-woodsy or unsophisticated things might happen if we permitted our worship to get "carried away" like this.

I'm not minimizing the potential complexity of welcoming this kind of movement in worship. And perhaps it's just too far outside the mainline church worship culture to be something that could be emotionally authentic (i.e. mark five) for us. But at the very least, I wonder what a progressive Christian experience of this kind of "adventuring in the Holy Spirit" might look like. I can't help but wonder if there are fresh "waves of Spirit" that God would long for us to catch in our progressive Christian worship if we were willing to look for them, wait for them, and ride them when they arrive.

MUSIC AND LITURGY

In many ways what we're really talking about here is how to make sure our music serves and fits our liturgy. The word "liturgy" literally means "the work of the people." It's the word we use to describe our "order of service" in worship, and it refers to the things that the community does together in the process of worshipping God.

In the churches in which worship leaders like Matt Redman minister, the liturgy usually begins with a lengthy time of singing and praying. The song leaders are given an open-ended (usually 15-30 minutes or so) time at the beginning of the service in which to praise God through song and create an atmosphere in which people can pour out their hearts in prayer and praise in spontaneous ways. They may sing six or more songs in a row, and if something "happens" along the lines of what Matt Redman was describing, they allow the Spirit to take over and lead them wherever the

Spirit wants to go—even if it means singing much longer than the leaders had originally planned. This is part of their worship culture. They are open to having the Spirit break in and do something completely unexpected.

Worship leaders in this tradition develop a great sense of timing and skill when it comes to gradually building the intensity of the congregation's focus on God's presence. They deliberately make sure that they give themselves time and permission to help create an atmosphere in which people can truly worship in their more emotional, spontaneous, and open-ended ways.

In most mainline or traditional churches, our liturgies are obviously quite different from what I've just described. We tend to have an "opening hymn" or one song, followed by a spoken call to worship, a written unison prayer of some kind, then perhaps another song, etc. Our liturgies tend to be more scripted, more reserved, and more controlled. In most of our congregations there is, as a preaching professor of mine (Rev. Ernest Campbell) once joked, "an assumption that the Holy Spirit never moves after sixty minutes," and that "a service does not need to be everlasting to have eternal significance!"

I am not suggesting that worship needs to go on forever, and while the "sixty minute expectation" can be constricting and frustrating, some good cases can be made for trying to be clear and respectful regarding time parameters, etc. But the main point here is to ask ourselves whether or not our liturgical traditions and structures are somehow boxing us in and preventing us from being fully open to the Spirit. Do we feel as though we have been granted permission as worship leaders to truly listen for and respond to the Holy Spirit's unscripted leading? What would it look like in a more mainline or traditional liturgy for us to be open to the Sprit "breaking in" and taking us on an unexpected journey?

John van de Laar shares a powerful example of a highly respected mainline preacher responding to the Spirit in the context of a traditional mainline worship service in an unscripted and unanticipated way;

In 1931 William Temple was leading a congregation in the University church of St. Mary the Virgin at the end of what was known as the Oxford

Mission. During the singing of the hymn "When I Survey The Wondrous Cross," he stopped the music just before the last stanza, and encouraged the people to read the words to themselves silently. Then, he invited those who could sing with whole-hearted commitment, to sing the words loudly. Those who did not feel they could commit to the words, he invited to remain silent, and those who felt they could mean the words only a little, and who wanted to grow in their commitment to them, he asked to sing in a whisper. With that, the organ began to play again, and the whisper of two thousand voices was heard singing:

Were the whole realm of nature mine
That were an offering far too small
Love so amazing, so divine,
Demands my soul, my life, my all.

This experience was not forgotten by those who were present.[7]

Tension Between Some "Praise and Worship" Songs and Mainline Church Liturgy

In my experience, one of the reasons why some of the attempts in mainline congregations to use praise and worship songs often fall flat—apart from any of the issues covered by the six marks—is that we are trying to simply "plop" a contemporary song into a liturgical form that does not give that song an opportunity to offer what it was created to offer. Some of those songs, for example, were written to be the fourth or fifth song that a congregation might sing in its opening time of six consecutive songs. There is a style, intensity, and depth to the song's music and lyric that would not work well as an "opening hymn" in a traditional liturgy. The song might not really "do its magic" if it was not immediately preceded or followed by another song that helped to set it up.

Worship leaders I have known in more evangelical churches put a great deal of time and energy into choosing songs that deliberately take the worshipping community on a "journey of praise." There is a deliberate way of starting off—perhaps singing a song that helps folks to simply gather and "enter the gates"—and then they build and move and have a deliberate destination in mind—perhaps ending up before the "throne of Grace" in wide open passionate adoration of God. But they don't start off with passionate adoration. They give themselves some time to get there. As a talented worship leader (whose name I cannot remember!) put it years ago in a seminar I attended,

> I'm not ready to sing, "Holy, Holy, Holy" when I first enter the sanctuary. I need to let go of all the other stuff on my mind first. Or I might need to get over the argument I had with my kids or my wife on the way to church! Let me sing, "We Gather Together," and catch my breath. Let me first just enter into the 'courts of praise,' and then help me get to the place at which I'm ready to stand wide open before God and dare to sing, "Holy, Holy, Holy."

I am not in any way suggesting that more traditional churches need to scrap our liturgies or try to adopt the liturgical structures of more evangelical congregations (though if a community is led by the Spirit to do so there's nothing wrong with that). But what I am suggesting is that our song choices need to fit our liturgies. The purpose of our music is to help us do whatever it is we are attempting to do together in worship. The songs we bring into worship need to be able to "work" in the context of their liturgical moment.

So if we are not going to have twenty minutes or so of open-ended musical worship at the beginning of our service, then we probably do not want to sing one song that was actually created for that kind of liturgical experience. If we're going to start with one opening song, then we want to use a song that will serve that purpose and stand alone well. This does not mean that we have to use a traditional hymn necessarily, though that may well be the best choice for a given congregation.

But one of the main reasons I'm writing this book is to let folks know that there are many new "contemporary hymns and songs" being created and released that will indeed serve more traditional church liturgies. And, many congregations are now beginning to encourage and empower their own musicians to write music for worship that will fit their own context and liturgical structure perfectly. That's fantastic!

So let's get clear on what it is we are called to do in our services of worship, use and/or create new liturgies that help us to worship as meaningfully as possible, and find or create the music we need to serve our liturgical structures and goals.

Chapter 7: Questions For Discussion

1. Take a look once again at the list of things that Bryan suggested that worship helps us to experience and/or do. (listed here as well as in the chapter itself). Does anything in this list jump out to you as particularly significant? Is there anything you disagree with? Are there important aspects of worship which are not in this list?

Worship is About:

a. Deliberately focusing our awareness and attention on the presence and beauty of God; intentionally expressing heart-felt love, appreciation, and gratitude to God for the gift of life and for the joy of knowing and experiencing God's "Being;" creating "thin places" in which worshippers encounter God in life-changing and transforming ways.

b. Regaining our spiritual focus and "coming back home" to God if and when we've somehow wandered away. It's about finding our bearings again and re-grounding our beings in the One who matters most and in the relationships and aspects of life that matter most.

c. Helping us to look beyond ourselves—getting beyond the private agendas and schemes that so easily become self-serving and other-harming—moving beyond our small stories and stepping back into God's larger Story as revealed to us through scripture.

d. Helping us to find release from our insecurities and fears; putting our trust in God and finding our true security in God.

e. Finding comfort and healing in times of great sadness and heavy burdens.

f. Responding again and again to God's love for us. Being reminded that the best way we can live out our gratitude to God is by offering ourselves—all we are and all we have—back to God, and by committing ourselves (or recommitting ourselves) to living lives of loving service to others.

g. Helping us renew our commitment to working with other people in community. Being empowered by the Holy Spirit to make God's Dream of justice and peace for the world and all of creation a present reality.

2. Can you think of songs that have helped you experience or do some of the things listed above in the context of worship?

3. Do you have a renewed sense of the importance of the opportunity that is yours as one who helps choose and/or provide music for worship? In light of this, have you been giving your music ministry the time and energy that it really deserves? Perhaps you could close this discussion by praying for the help you need to renew your commitment to putting your heart and soul into your ministry of music.

4. What do you think of Matt Redman's remarks? Have you ever experienced this kind of "otherly moment" that he describes? Why do you think this kind of thing rarely (if ever!) happens in mainline or traditional or progressive congregations? Are we missing something? Is our understanding of worship completely different? Are there any opportunities in your worship services for God's Spirit to "break through" and take the worship experience someplace unexpected? What are the pros and cons of this? Do you feel encouraged and granted permission to listen for and to respond to the Spirit's leading in this regard?

5. What is the liturgical structure of your worship? Does your music serve the liturgy? Are there ways you'd like to change the liturgy if you could? What are some of the pros and cons of more open and spontaneous evangelical liturgies and the more scripted traditional liturgies of most mainline church traditions?

CHAPTER 8

Musical Styles And
The "Language of the Heart"

My friend Rich Wolfe, a UCC pastor in LaGrange, IL, said something about 20 years ago that I've never forgotten. We were having dinner with a few other colleagues and we were talking about some of the Contemporary Christian Music that was popular at that time.

At some point in the conversation Rich said, "I've learned to be a bit skeptical whenever I hear the word 'Christian' used as an adjective."

What a great statement.

I think of that remark almost every time I hear someone talk about "*Christian* music." I mean, what makes *music*—not the lyrics, but the music—"Christian?"

More recently I've heard well known pastor and author Rob Bell say, "Christian is a great noun, but a poor adjective." He'll probably be quoted more often than my friend Rich, but Rich was obviously thinking along these lines many years ago.

MUSIC IS MUSIC

As far as I'm concerned, music is music. I'm referring to music without lyrics. There is nothing uniquely or particularly or essentially "Christian" about any one type of music. Sure, there are many different styles and kinds of music. I may personally enjoy some of them more than others.

Some styles of music tend to "speak" to me more than others, which is to say that they somehow move me or touch my heart or evoke a certain mood or feeling. I might say that some kinds of music tend to be more "pleasing to my ears" than others.

Likewise, some voices or instruments or instrumental ensembles are more appealing to me than others. But this is a totally subjective and personal thing, and it also depends on my mood and on the reasons why I am choosing to listen to a certain kind of instrument and music at a particular time and place. The point I'm making here is simply that we've all got our own personal preferences when it comes to music, and these preferences say more about who *we* are than they do about the quality or essence of the music itself.

To put it mildly, there are an awful lot of strong opinions in the world regarding styles of music, and this is definitely true when it comes to the music we experience in churches! Differing opinions about musical style, the appropriate role and place of music in worship, and how these decisions should be made are often at the center of painful undercurrents, disagreements, and divisions in churches. It's an area in which we church-going folks tend to be extremely hard on each other. At times we can be flat out mean-spirited, arrogant, snobbish, judgmental, and way too full of ourselves.

I wouldn't be at all surprised if some of you reading this have been the focus of criticism in your worshipping community because you've tried to bring a new style of music into the life of your congregation.

It's amazing how many ego, control, and power issues get played out in congregations when it comes to music. Even choices regarding the song melodies that ring from church carillons can be sources of conflict! If this book does little more than help you and others you work with realize that you might need to take a deeper look at your own egos and control issues in connection with your music ministry (and we can *all* get snagged here from time to time!), it will have been well worth whatever price you paid for it.

The Problem With Sacred Vs. Secular

One of the main points I want to make in this chapter is that I think it's time for us to stop talking about one style of music being somehow more "sacred" or "Christian" than others. For that matter, there is no one style of music that is more "progressive" (in the way I'm using the word) than another either.

As has already been stated, music is music. We all have a right to our own preferences and opinions and experience. But we do not have a right to somehow "demonize" and/or exclude a style of music from worship simply because we do not personally care for it. There is no "devil's music," as conservative preachers used to refer to rock 'n roll, and there is no style or mode of music that is somehow essentially "Christian."

There is a difference between one's own personal taste and what is or is not "Godly."

I also don't believe it's legitimate to insist that a song is somehow more "sacred" or appropriate for worship because it mentions the name of God or Jesus or is "overtly spiritual." A song could be lyrically focused on a theme which is not considered to be conventionally "religious" at all, and yet it could be used by the Holy Spirit very powerfully to speak to the hearts of people in the context of worship.

As mentioned earlier in this book, the use of popular radio hits or other so-called secular songs in worship can be profoundly effective. A pastor friend of mine recently shared with me that her congregation sang U2's "When Love Came To Town" for a Palm Sunday service and that it was deeply moving and served their liturgical purposes perfectly. Beautiful.

Why Have *New* Music In A Worship Service at All?

It might be helpful to stop and ask ourselves why so many churches these days are experimenting with more current musical styles in the context of worship. There are probably some good reasons for this, and also some reasons that aren't very solid at all. One of the not-so-good reasons as far as I'm concerned is in order to *compete* with other churches in a community.

I think you probably know what I'm alluding to here. What often happens is that there is some newer congregation in the area that is growing like crazy, and maybe even "stealing some sheep" from the traditional churches in town. Pastors and leaders of the traditional churches start wondering what's going on in these newer congregations that people—especially younger people—are finding so attractive and compelling.

Eventually, it's discovered that these new churches have rock bands instead of organs and traditional church music programs, and that they are singing contemporary praise and worship music instead of traditional hymns. So in an attempt to compete with these growing churches, the traditional churches get a band together and try to be a bit more contemporary in their style of worship music. They might start an additional service which they refer to as "contemporary worship" or something like that.

The assumption at work is that people are attending these other churches because the worship style is more entertaining and less "churchy." The problem however is that most of these attempts on the part of mainline church folks to mirror the worship style of the fast-growing independent churches in the area just don't "work."

It's not that bringing new music into the church isn't necessarily a good idea. I've spent the majority of my adult life doing just that! But if it's being done in order to be more "with the times" or primarily in order to compete with other churches, etc., then chances are it will somehow fall short of the desired result. The passion will be missing. The authenticity will be missing. The spirit will be missing. It just won't quite feel right. If it's more about marketing or trying to be perceived as a church that is "culturally relevant" than it is about worshipping God with passion and depth, people will sense the difference.

So let me be blunt. I think the reason many folks these days are leaving traditional churches and going to more evangelical churches with "contemporary worship" is not primarily because they like the style of music in these new churches. It's not primarily because these churches have "dumbed down" the Gospel and made complex issues more black and white and thus more appealing to people who don't want to have to deal with paradox and ambiguity (though that may sometimes be the case).

I think it's primarily because these other churches are often doing a better job of helping people enter into and nurture a meaningful, life-changing, and hope-filled relationship with the God of the Bible. We may not agree with their theology or with their understanding and interpretation of the biblical Story, but we need to be humble enough to admit that these churches are often doing a better job than we are of helping people enter into a life of faith that is compelling and life-changing.

When it comes to worship, these churches often "feel more alive" than we do in our traditional modes of worship. That's not just about being "happy clappy," getting a "Jesus buzz," or reducing the faith to emotionalism (recall chapter 5). It's about people being enthused about their own relationship with God—having "something to sing about"—and welcoming a sense of celebration and excitement in worship.

Rev. Peter Gomes said something during an address he gave in Hartford, CT on the occasion of the 50th anniversary of the United Church of Christ that connects well with the point I'm making here. He was talking about the exponential growth of Pentecostal churches throughout the entire world in recent decades, and he shared with the gathering that he was convinced that the real key to this growth is that Pentecostal Christians "are not embarrassed by joy."[1]

People want and need an experience of faith and worship that is worth celebrating. There's no one way to celebrate, but if our worship is so solemn that it feels more like a funeral than a party, we should not wonder why many of our members—especially the younger members—eventually lose interest.

After traveling around the country and worshipping in over 1000 congregations for more than 25 years of full-time itinerant music ministry, I'm convinced that congregations grow in healthy ways not because of the style with which they worship, but because the church is helping people to experience God's transforming and healing Love.

People want and need to be fed spiritually. There is a profound spiritual longing in our culture at this point in history. Many people are hungry for an experience of spiritual community that will help them to connect with God and live lives of spiritual integrity. If they are inclined to look for this in the form of a Christian community, they are searching for worship experiences that will help them make sense of the chaos and emptiness and brokenness in their own lives and in this world. They want to know that they are forgiven when they mess up, and that there is hope when things seem hopeless. They want to know that they are loved and that there is a group of people who are committed to caring for them and being there for them when the bottom falls out or when it all hits the fan. They want worship that will help them mature spiritually and keep on track and help them find and use their gifts. They want worship that engages their heart as well as their intellect. They want to be challenged to follow the teachings of Scripture and to live for more than just their own personal well-being or a bigger piece of the materialistic pie. In other words, they want a church that is serious about "being church." Please trust me—a "hip style of music" will not make these things happen! No *style* of music will make these things happen in and of itself.

So once again, it's important to return to the reason why we have music of any kind in church in the first place, and that is in order to help us worship God and to experience God's presence in community more fully. To me, the key questions to ask ourselves are, "How can we help folks in our congregation worship God with passion, and integrity?" "How can we help people 'sing their hearts out' with an authentic sense of joy and celebration?" "What kind of music will help our congregation offer heart-felt worship to God, and what kind of music will help our congregation as a whole do whatever it is we are trying to do liturgically at a given point in the worship service?"

If the answers to these questions are that the older traditional music of the church is no longer speaking deeply enough to the hearts and minds of the people gathered, or that more contemporary music will help folks to connect with and experience God's presence more deeply, or that people are longing to sing songs that help them express their longing for God in fresh ways that ring true theologically and artistically in today's culture and context, then these would all be some great reasons to try to worship God in and through some new music. Yes, this will hopefully draw more people to these worship services, but that is because the music is helping folks to connect with God deeply—not because it's hip or cool or contemporary.

THE TRADITIONAL MUSIC MAY BE WORKING JUST FINE!

It's also important to understand that there are many congregations in which the traditional music *is* fully serving its purpose of helping the folks of that community to worship beautifully. When and where this is the case, there may be no compelling reason to introduce new contemporary styles of music at all.

As we're about to explore even further, Progressive Christian Worship Music is not about the "style" of the music—it's about making sure that the music being used is helping the people of a congregation to worship as meaningfully as possible. That will depend upon the congregation.

I have recently learned of a new church start (The ELCA Lutheran "House For All Sinners And Saints" in Denver, CO) that is very progressive and cutting edge and growing rapidly, and yet they sing only traditional hymns without any instrumental accompaniment whatsoever. They find meaning in connecting with previous generations and the Holy Spirit by singing the historic hymns of the Church, and by worshipping in and through the music that can only be made with human breath and bodies. Fantastic! Who knows—perhaps the unique combination of progressive theology and traditional liturgy that is at the heart of their worship life would be tragically derailed if they started using contemporary musical forms and instrumentation. The whole point is to help the congregation worship powerfully in ways that are authentic and right for that community—not to force a particular style of music into places in which it is neither needed nor desired.

MUSIC AND THE HEART LANGUAGE
OF THE CONGREGATION

Any kind of music can be used for worship depending on the congregation. I trust I've made that point clearly enough, but I want you to know that I really do mean *any* kind of music—jazz, rap, country, rock, metal, rhythm and blues, techno, gospel, classical, industrial, music from any ethnic tradition—there are no limits as long as the music is being used to help those gathered in a particular time and place to worship God.

While all styles of music are fair game for worship, however, and while musical style alone should not be the starting point for decisions made about what kind of music we use in church, the simple truth is that one of the main reasons I'm writing this book is because there are huge numbers of people in traditional churches these days who long for new worship music that is theologically more progressive and stylistically more "contemporary."

In other words, increasing numbers of progressive Christians are hungry for worship music with lyrics that ring true and music that "moves them." For a lot of people, traditional church music, and organ music in particular, is at best something that they have *learned* to respect and appreciate even though it doesn't really appeal to them emotionally or aesthetically.

So what these people are wanting is some music in the context of worship that feels more accessible to them and that has the power to move their hearts.

Music—just the music—without lyrics—can move a person or a group in ways that are literally beyond verbal description. Music can speak directly to the human heart as few other things do, and when we sensitively combine powerful music with soulful lyrics, we can create songs that have the capacity to speak to human hearts *and* minds in ways that are profound, life changing, and as composer Richard Bruxvoort-Colligan puts it, "world making."

I can't even count the times over the years that someone has said something like this to me; "I've always known and believed what you helped us to sing about, but when you put it to music, it touched me in a way that it never did without the music."

This power to "touch" people—to "move" people—to get deep down to the "heart of things" is one of the main reasons why we use music in worship. In many traditional worship services, music may be just about the only place in the liturgy where we deliberately welcome the presence and participation of our emotions. Music somehow speaks, as one of my favorite singer/songwriters David Wilcox puts it, the "language of the heart."

So what we're really aiming at here is some new music that will speak the "heart language" of the people who are gathered for worship.

If there is a specific style of music that helps a congregation worship in its own *collective* heart language, then by all means that style should be embraced and celebrated and used often and with gusto—whatever it is. Predominantly African-American congregations for example may primarily use "Gospel music" in their worship because the sound and style of this music speaks the "heart language" of most of the members of the worshipping community. Wonderful.

There may be worshipping communities in which Bach, Mozart, and classical music in general speaks the heart language of the majority of folks in the congregation. Beautiful. There may be other communities in which blue grass or country or jazz would speak the heart language of the vast majority of congregants. Then those styles should be embraced and used in worship often if at all possible.

It may be however that one of the key problems many churches are now having is that they are "sticking with" a style of church music that no longer speaks the heart language of the majority of those gathered for worship. If and when this is the case, we are robbing the community of music's God-given power to help worshippers praise, experience, connect with, and respond to God. This is tragic and completely unnecessary.

That last paragraph is worth reading again.

Of course it may also be the case that there *is no one primary musical heart language* in a particular congregation.

The congregation may be so diverse (a beautiful thing!) that different kinds of music will be needed to help different folks worship more deeply. In this case there's probably no way to please everyone at the same time, and maybe the best we can do is include lots of different musical styles in worship in an attempt to honor the diversity of musical heart languages that are present in a circle of worshippers.

For that matter, it may be a beautiful thing to deliberately sing songs from musical traditions and cultures that are *not* the primary heart language of a given group of people as a way of reminding the congregation that God's Rainbow of Love is huge and includes all colors and styles and traditions.

But what we're really searching for is music that the whole congregation can sing together—which will help them worship God as one body—that communicates in the heart language of the worshipping community.

CHAPTER 8: QUESTIONS FOR DISCUSSION

1. What did you think about Rev. Rich Wolfe's statement, "I've learned to be a bit skeptical whenever I hear the word 'Christian' used as an adjective?"

2. What are some of the styles of music (just music without lyrics) or instruments that tend to move your heart most deeply? Is there a style of music that tends to put you in a "worshipful posture" more than others? Are these musical styles and/or instruments a part of your congregation's worship music? If not, why not?

3. Reflect a bit together on Bryan's statement, "There is a difference between one's own personal taste and what is or is not "Godly."

4. Have you experienced attempts to bring "contemporary music" into a worship service that just did not seem to work? What was missing? What about times when it *did* work? What seemed to make the difference?

5. What do you think about Rev. Peter Gomes statement that Pentecostal churches are growing exponentially because Pentecostal Christians are not "embarrassed by joy?" Is there enough focus or room for joy and celebration in your worship? What is the difference between joy and getting "pumped up with giddy feelings?" Is it important for worship to somehow give us a lift emotionally and spiritually or to help us to "feel better?" If so, how can music help with this?

6. Reflect a bit together on Bryan's statement that mainline or traditional churches sometimes lose members to more evangelical churches because these churches are often doing a better job of inviting people into an experience of faith that is meaningful and alive and transforming. Do you agree? Disagree?

7. Do traditional hymns speak the heart language of your congregation? Chances are they sometimes do and they sometimes don't. What makes the difference? Can you think of a time when your heart was

profoundly moved by a traditional hymn? Share some of these with each other.

8. Is there a musical style that you think would definitely speak the "heart language" of your congregation? If there are several, what might they be, and how can you honor this diversity and deal with it?

CHAPTER 9

Worship, Performance, And Ego Work

Since the purpose of worship music is to help the congregation to focus on, experience, and respond to God, then it should go without saying that we musicians and worship leaders need to be extremely careful regarding the role of our own egos in the context of worship. Anyone who is at all self-aware, honest, and musically gifted knows how difficult this can be!

But to be quite straightforward, worship is not about us and our gifts. It's about God.

Worship is *not* the time or place to try to blow people away with our musical chops or virtuosity or even with *our gifts for leading others in worship*. Of course at the same time we want to use all of our best gifts and skills and energy to help the community worship. We want to be excellent worship leaders. But we don't want the attention to be on our excellence.

Easier said than done.

I imagine we've all had experiences of church music that were somehow more about musicians showing off than about helping the entire congregation to sing together with hearts focused on God. It's not too hard to sense when a musician is just a little too full of him or herself. This goes for choir directors and choirs as well as individual musicians.

In fact, Professor Christopher Grundy often observes that the original purpose of church choirs was not to sing *for* or *to* a congregation. Rather, it was to help the congregation sing![1] It's amazing how much this has been completely turned around in so many congregations.

On the other hand, most of us have also had experiences of music in church in which the skill of a musician or a choir actually *did* enhance our experience of God's beauty and presence and love.

I'm not in agreement with those who suggest that there is no place for performance or for "solos" at all in church. If that were the case, then we'd need to do away with preaching altogether, because it is also a solo art form, and can just as easily descend into an individual preacher "peacocking" his or her gifts as opposed to leading others in worship.

I think there is indeed a place in worship for musicians to "play skillfully" as it says in Psalm 33:3. Individual excellence and virtuosity can glorify God instead of just causing listeners to be impressed with the gifts of the musician. I don't think it serves our worship of God necessarily when we deliberately diminish our gifts in the name of being humble or "giving God the glory." That's often some kind of false humility.

So how and where do we draw the line between musicians showing off our gifts in ego-driven ways, and musicians glorifying God with the gifts that the Creator has entrusted to us? It all comes down I think to the hearts and attitudes of the musicians. Ultimately, this is one of those things that a congregation can feel. Who we are at our core will communicate more than anything we say, especially over time.

It's usually rather obvious when someone is *using worship* as a chance to show off, and it's also usually quite obvious when a person is *sharing a gift* in order to help the congregation worship. All we musicians can do is constantly monitor our own egos (without doing so much introspection that we are driving ourselves and others crazy or actually just giving our egos a chance to get caught being impressed with how "ego-free" we are!) and do our part to keep our hearts in the right place.

When our hearts *are* in the right place, people can sense it. And that is something that begins long before a worship service starts and long after the service concludes. If we're ego driven in the rest of life, it's just not going to work to try to be a humble servant when we put on our "worship leader hat." That won't pass the smell test.

But when we've done our inner ego work, then we are free to offer the fullness of our gifts in all of their God-given glory. Then we can play or sing our hearts out and people will still know that this is not about us trying to call attention to ourselves. Maybe the best way to safeguard against ego-stroking in the name of worship music is to make sure that we musicians are, ourselves, truly worshipping God as we share our music. I'm not talking about looking a certain way—you know—closing our eyes and doing our best to look as though we are "having a moment" with God—I'm talking about offering the music to God from the bottom of our hearts in whatever ways are authentic for us. Again, when it's for real, people usually know it and feel it.

One more thing, and this is really important to grasp. When we are truly flowing in our gifts and call to lead congregational music, we may also sometimes choose to *deliberately decrease our own role in a song* so that the congregation can sing together more fully. This is not a matter of false humility or of diminishing our gifts. It is a matter of maturely owning our primary purpose as musical worship leaders, and that is to help the congregation worship in song together. This could take the form of song leaders with microphones deliberately stepping away from their mics once the congregation has learned a song so that the congregation can hear itself as one voice rather than be drowned out or dominated by the singers with the mics. This isn't easy for folks to do, especially when the singers with mics have beautiful voices that people in the congregation love to hear.

Ego, Control, and Musical Leadership

As I mentioned earlier in this book, a lot of ego and turf and control issues tend to get played out in churches when it comes to the whole area of music. I'm sure I'm not telling you anything you don't already know here! But it's important for us to look at this, name it for what it is—especially within ourselves—and do whatever inner work we need to do in order to let God's Spirit lead us, heal the pain connected to the conflicts that emerge out of these ego conflicts, and teach us how to lead without dominating and/or controlling.

I know—this is so much easier said than done. And yet nothing is more important. Nothing will take the life out of a music ministry more than unrecognized and unresolved ego issues. This stuff is toxic if and when it is not owned and lovingly dealt with. And it can be so subtle.

I don't have any magic formulas for how to stay in touch with our own ego issues, but I will say this. Each of us needs to do our *own* work here. So often when I find myself getting annoyed with someone else for being too controlling or ego-driven, what is really going on is that I'm projecting my own ego or control needs onto that other person. The real issue may be that *I* don't agree with someone else's choices or preferences, and that *I* want to have my own way because *I* somehow know better, etc. After all, this is *my* area of expertise and *I'm* more trained and experienced and *I've* been here "in the trenches" doing this work much longer and *I* know this church and people better than he or she does and they should be listening to *me!*

Sound at all familiar?

But rather than deal with the fact that I'm having a hard time letting go of my own sense of what should be happening, I blame someone else for insisting that *his* or *her* choices or preferences are correct or more important. And that other person may be doing exactly the same thing. Round and round we go.

At the same time, it's important for us to acknowledge that some people are uniquely called and gifted to be in positions of musical leadership in congregations. These leaders should be encouraged to own what my friend Gordon Cosby calls "their inner authority" when it comes to their area of call and gift. We need to acknowledge who our musical leaders are, and not only respect their leadership, but actually encourage them to lead us.

In the name of trying to be good team players and ego-free leaders, it's possible for us to sometimes relinquish our own inner authority in ways that will not serve an event or a worship service or a congregation at all. I know I have done this at times. It's another form of false humility. There are times when what we really need is to honor our own instincts and gifts and, as lovingly as possible, insist that this is one of those times when we need our team members to just "trust us (or me)."

Of course there is no guarantee that any of us will always be unambiguously "right," even when we've insisted that others need to trust us and take our lead! But if and when our instincts are somehow off, we will be given yet another opportunity to deal with our own egos as we admit that things didn't go as well as we'd hoped! These will usually be good lessons for everyone, and if all the members of a band or worship team (including pastors) are doing their ego work, the entire team's ability to lead the congregation in song will be enhanced by being willing to humbly learn from what does *not* work as well as what does.

So how do we balance these things out?

By nurturing our own inner lives in prayer and whatever other spiritual disciplines and practices help us to stay centered in the Spirit. By communicating openly and lovingly with others with whom we are working to serve the congregation's worship in the area of music. By being mature and gracious enough to admit when we realize our egos have gotten the best of us once again—which they will! This is a lifelong process and none of us will ever fully "arrive" at a place of total ego freedom.

And I think we also need to be able to have a sense of humor, smile at all of this, not take ourselves too seriously, and just accept the fact that we're going to blow it from time to time.

WHO CHOOSES YOUR MUSIC?

So let's make sure the rubber meets the road here. Many of the ego and power issues that get played out in the area of church music come down to who has the authority—the final word—when it comes to choosing the songs that will be used in worship.

Some pastors have strong feelings here. They may have been trained to believe that as pastors they are the ones who are ultimately responsible for everything that happens in worship, including song choices. There are full-time ministers of music in congregations however who were also trained to assume that *they* have the final word regarding musical choices in worship. I know of one young graduate from a choir college who flat out told his pastor that all musical choices belonged to him and that he would not tolerate any pastoral interference in this domain. You can guess how well that approach worked . . .

There are organists who have played in congregations for decades and who have always assumed that it was completely up to them to choose the music for worship. There are praise and worship bands that have clearly defined leaders who bring the music to rehearsals, and there are bands in which all the members are encouraged to help choose the songs they use in worship. The point I'm making here is that there is no one way to approach this issue regarding who has the authority to choose music for worship.

At the same time, pastors and church musicians often have very strong opinions when it comes to all of this. So clear and respectful communication is essential here! Pray for the Spirit's presence and guidance, love each other with the love of Christ, do your own ego work, bring your most mature self to the table, and get into this conversation together.

Personally, I prefer collaborative approaches to deciding what music to use, and for all persons involved to know that their opinions and preferences and perspectives are valued and needed and that they make a difference. I prefer shared authority in virtually all areas of congregational life. I prefer worship teams (dare I say committees?) to worship czars. But I also understand that it is necessary in some cases for specific leaders to be recognized and respected and encouraged to make decisions and even to have the "final word" in certain areas. I am among those who were taught in seminary that if the pastor did not have *the* final word regarding "all things worship," he or she should at least be a key member of whatever circle of folks will be making decisions regarding congregational worship. I was taught that worship is an area in which pastors are trained and called to bring some serious "inner authority" to a congregation. That still makes sense to me. But the simple truth is that some pastors are clueless when it comes to music, worship music, and how music can make or break a liturgical moment. It's just not their gift in some cases. It sure helps greatly when pastors who do not have a good feel for music are mature and ego-free enough to admit this and to make sure that gifted music leaders are on the worship team.

The point is to be clear, deliberate, Christ-centered, and loving in the process of deciding which songs you will use in your worship music. My hope and prayer for you is that the *process* of choosing your music will reflect what the music itself is all about—worshipping God and loving each other. Do your ego work. Own your own inner authority. Honor and encourage the gifts of your leaders and of each team member. Let God's Spirit melt your hearts and heal hurt feelings and resentments if and when they emerge—and they will.

DON'T GIVE MEDIOCRITY AN EXCUSE TO FLOURISH

Let me just say here finally that I think it's crucially important for church musicians to work hard to be the best musicians and worship leaders we can possibly be. Too often, especially with "praise and worship bands," I've heard people justify or excuse mediocre or even lousy musicianship by saying, "well, this is about worship and not performance anyway."

Please don't do this.

One extremely gifted pastor once told me that when it comes to music in their worship, they are a "pro-participation/anti-excellence congregation." I understand what she meant, but again, I don't think that "excellence" is the problem.

Yes, if we have to choose between excellent musicians who are stuck up and poor musicians who are humble and who love God, we'll take the latter. There are times when someone's very lack of polish and overt skill may somehow be used by the Spirit in a beautiful and tender way to emphasize that "this is about God, not performance." But this is almost always an unnecessary choice, and the simple truth is that any kind of church music that is done poorly can actually distract folks from being able to focus on worshipping God.

The less the music is somehow *about* the musicians, and the more it is about leading the congregation into an experience of worshipping God, the better. Poor musicianship can put the focus on the musician every bit as much as the excellence of "stars" who are too impressed with their own ability.

CHAPTER 9: QUESTIONS FOR DISCUSSION

1. What do you think about Christopher Grundy's comment that historically, the original purpose of a choir was not to sing *for* the congregation, but to help the congregation sing? If you have a choir, is it being used in this way? If you have a worship band, the same could be said of its purpose. Do you sing *for* the congregation, or help the congregation sing? Would the members of the congregation have the same answer to the previous question as you do? How can you be even more deliberate about helping the congregation to sing? How do microphones for singers impact this?

2. How do you deliberately stay in touch with your own ego issues when it comes to your life and your music ministry in particular? This may be tough to admit, but are there ways in which you need to own the fact that you've been overly controlling in your musical leadership?

3. Bryan mentioned the importance of encouraging those who are called and gifted to offer musical leadership to own their own "inner authority." Have you ever given your inner authority away inappropriately? Have you ever seen someone else do this? How can you best acknowledge and trust those in your congregation who are truly called and gifted to lead when it comes to music?

4. Are there any undercurrents of ego and/or control in your congregation's music ministry that you feel you need to name and deal with? If so, what kind of process is needed for this to happen in a healthy and constructive way? Focus on your own ego issues, and for now don't worry about others.

5. What is the process by which the songs you sing in worship are chosen? Who has this authority in your congregation? Are you all on the same page here? This can be awkward, but have whatever conversation you need to have in order to communicate clearly and respectfully about this. Is there one person in charge? A group? Can everyone have a voice that is heard and respected even if one person is ultimately the decision maker?

6. What did you think about Bryan's comments about the importance of not "giving mediocrity a chance to flourish?" How do you balance the importance of providing high quality musicianship while at the same time encouraging participation by those who may not be the "best" musicians but who have a sincere faith and a deep desire to share their gifts?

7. Is it hard for you to enter into to an experience of worship yourself when you are in the process of leading the congregation? What can you do to be able to actually worship as you are also trying to help others do the same?

8. Spend some time in prayer together asking God to show you if and when your egos are in the way, and asking God to help you do this never-ending ego work with grace and integrity and a sense of humor. Ask the Spirit to help those of you who provide musical leadership in your congregation to humbly work together as cooperatively and lovingly as possible.

CHAPTER 10

Some Thoughts About Worship Songs

INDIVIDUAL WORSHIP AND GROUP WORSHIP

I've had some life-changing and incredibly sweet experiences of worship by myself, and I hope you have too. My relationship with God is a very intimate thing, and there are times when worship is what "happens" between God and me alone. Some of my most cherished and beautiful musical worship experiences have been times when I've sung my heart out to God all by myself with no one else around.

But this book is about music that we *sing in community*. As you'll recall from chapter four, one of the key marks of Progressive Christian Worship Music is that it will deliberately take us beyond the individualism that is at the heart of a lot of contemporary praise and worship music.

So one of the key points I want to make now is that when we sing in church, we are singing as a community—as one collective body. It's not just about "Jesus and me." It's about Jesus, God, and *us*, and it's about music that folks of all ages can sing together.

SOLO SONGS VS. WORSHIP SONGS

When I started my music ministry, I was primarily writing solo material that I would perform for folks to listen to. I learned (mostly the hard way by what didn't work!) that writing songs for groups to sing together is a very different art form altogether.

In a solo song, I say things *as I would say them* without needing to wonder if what I'm saying could authentically be "put into the mouths" of everyone gathered. I write melodies that are easy or fun for *me* to sing without regard to whether or not others can easily sing along.

But when I write songs for worship, then it's not just about what works for me. I'm thinking instead of whether or not everyone gathered will want to sing the words of the song, and whether or not the words and the music will help others to worship God. I make sure that the key and melody range is as accessible as possible to the greatest number of people. I sometimes simplify the syncopation so that folks aren't struggling with too many notes and words. I make sure that there are not difficult intervals that will make the song overly challenging for others to sing. In other words, I do my best to make the songs "singable" by as many people as possible.

If this book had been titled "Progressive Christian Music," instead of "The 6 Marks of Progressive Christian Worship Music," it would be a completely different book. I'd probably be focusing primarily on the music of Christians who have been singing about justice and peace and inclusivity and compassion for the poor, etc. (i.e. singing about progressive Christian themes) as solo artists.

But music composed for group worship tends to be very different from music written to be sung by an individual. The whole purpose is to bring the people together so that they become "one communal voice."

Sometimes a song that was originally written as a solo piece can be used in worship and can be sung by the entire congregation. Some songs will work both ways. As was stated previously, there is nothing wrong with using a familiar solo radio hit in worship if it somehow helps the congregation do what it is gathered to do at a given point in a worship service. I actually love this use of popular music, as long as it's done well and truly helps folks to worship.

But generally, group worship songs will be different from songs written to be sung by an individual performer and simply listened to by everyone else. The focus and content of the lyrics will often be different. The structure of the song will usually not involve "bridges" the way solo songs often do. Again, it's all about making the songs accessible enough for groups of people to be able to sing well together in the context of worship. The challenge for composers of new songs in this genre lies in creating songs that are both accessible to the majority of the people gathered *and* artistically compelling. That's no small task . . .

ELEMENTS OF A GOOD PROGESSIVE CHRISTIAN WORSHIP SONG

This is by no means an exclusive check list for a good worship song, and as always, lists like these on my part are intended to be a guide and not a legalistic test. But here is a recap of some of what I've been pointing toward in this chapter that I hope will be helpful.

A good progressive Christian worship song will:

1. **Be musically appealing** (be something that we are attracted to musically—music that speaks the heart language of the group as much as possible—music that moves us and/or somehow touches our hearts)

2. **Serve the liturgy** (help the entire congregation do whatever it is being led to do together at a given moment in the worship service—praise, celebrate, confess, lament, pray, reflect, prepare for a sermon, respond to a biblical text, find courage, prepare for a sacrament, commission members to engage in mission, etc.)

3. **Have lyrical content that helps the whole congregation to worship** (have a message that is in line with the 6 Marks and that helps the congregation do some of the things we alluded to in chapter seven). And what are those 6 Marks again?

    i. Praise, Justice, and the Full Range of Human Experience

    ii. Inclusive Language

iii. Progressive Theology

iv. Both the Individual and the Community

v. Emotional Authenticity

vi. Fresh Image, Ideas, and Language

4. **Be "singable"**

a. Have a melody that is easy to sing—not too much difficult syncopation or too many difficult intervals or too many words that are difficult for folks of all ages to keep up with. Worship songs usually don't have "bridges" the way pop songs or solo songs often do.

b. Be in an accessible key for the majority of voices—not have too many high or low notes that average singers can't reach. This is easier said than done, because different people have different ranges. But there *is* a range within which most people can sing . . . As a general rule, I no longer use high notes more than an octave above middle C. D tends to be a stretch for most—especially early in the morning!

PLEASE SING THE MELODY

This probably *should* go without saying, but in these days of American Idol and The Voice and all of the other talent shows that are currently popular, it's become fashionable for vocalists to show off their vocal ability by taking all kinds of liberties with the melody of songs. You know what I mean—it's done all the time by great singers when they sing The Star Spangled Banner at the beginning of sporting events. It's sometimes referred to as "vocal riffs and runs." It's very impressive and can be beautiful when done well, but most of us can't do it!

Please, when you are leading songs in worship, especially if it's a song which others in the congregation may not know—just sing the melody—the way it's written in notation or the way you'd like the congregation to learn it. If you are blessed with "riff and run" vocal ability, then set up a concert and we'll be glad to come and hear you do all that you're capable of doing. Or, if you're offering an anthem and are going to "riff up" Amazing Grace for us, that's great. But please just make sure you've done your ego work and that it's about glorifying God with your exceptional gifts and not about showing off your chops. As I said in the last chapter—people will know the difference.

But if you're trying to teach us a worship song, or lead the congregation in singing, then please sing the melody as you'd like the rest of us to learn it. We can't follow you or do what you're doing or even know what the melody is if you're all over the place with it, and as I've made clear by now, your purpose as a worship musician is to help the rest of us to sing the song.

Enough said about that!

THIS MUSIC IN NOT *JUST* FOR PROGRESSIVE CHRISTIANS

It feels important to simply acknowledge that in just about any congregation there are most likely going to be Christians present who do not consider themselves to be progressive in the ways that this book has been describing. Some of you are probably chuckling a bit to yourself now and thinking, "That's an understatement. The *majority* of the people in my church would not refer to themselves as 'progressive Christians.'" I understand this. Perhaps only the pastor and a small handful of folks in your congregation can fully embrace the 6 Marks of Progressive Christian Worship Music which this book describes.

But what I want you to know is that Progressive Christian Worship Music is not *just* for progressive Christians. There is no reason why more conservative Christians, in most cases, would not be able to sing Progressive Christian Worship Songs with passion and joy as well. Progressive Christian Worship Music is not about creating some special songs that progressive Christians will like and that conservative Christians will find offensive or unacceptable. In fact, when the songs are crafted well, conservative Christians may not even realize that there is anything "progressive" about Progressive Christian Worship Music. The music may emphasize aspects of the biblical vision which are not often emphasized in "praise and worship" music, but they are still all biblically grounded and about helping people to worship God.

You see the point is not to hit conservative Christians over the head with "progressive themes."

The point is to make sure that progressive Christians have great songs which help us worship God freely when we gather for that purpose—songs we don't have to spontaneously filter or edit in order to be able to sing with joyful abandon. We certainly hope and pray that Progressive Christian Worship songs will help *everyone gathered* in any worshipping context to praise, experience, and respond to God.

FINDING USABLE SONGS IN THE PRAISE AND WORSHIP INDUSTRY

As was mentioned in this book's first chapter, there are some great artists who are creating wonderful worship songs in the praise and worship world these days. It would be arrogant and just plain wrong to suggest that there are no songs coming out of that industry that are "worthy" of being used by progressive Christians. The problem is that very few if any of the artists in this genre are writing songs that would consistently line up with the 6 Marks of Progressive Christian Worship Music.

What a lot of more progressive pastors and musicians wind up doing is using some of these songs and then altering or substituting a word here or there that might need to be changed in order to make the language more inclusive for example. Unfortunately, it can take an awful lot of time to listen to praise and worship songs in order to find some that will "work" in more mainline worship contexts. And it can be rather tedious to have to filter through and make changes, etc.

So I'd like to point you toward a great resource here. I have a dear friend and colleague named Rev. Bob Wang.[1] Bob is a UCC pastor and an exceptionally talented musician and worship music leader. He has spent countless hours over the years listening to and keeping up with the best of contemporary praise and worship music. He has done the work of combing through these songs, deciding which ones are musically appealing, which ones have good theological content from a more mainline or progressive perspective, and which are the most "singable."

Bob welcomes you to contact him (see his e-mail address in the endnotes) and to have him share some of his favorite praise and worship songs with you. Because of copyright laws, he cannot offer a list of these songs in a book like this or on a website, so you'll need to be in conversation with him if you'd like to pick his brain and learn which songs he would recommend. In fact, Bob is available to come to congregations and offer workshops and consultations along these lines. I encourage you to be in touch with him.

CHAPTER 10: QUESTIONS FOR DISCUSSION

1. Try to think of a one or two of your favorite worship songs. What is it about this song that moves you and helps you to worship God?

2. Give an example of a worship song you know that is very easy to sing, and yet that has substance and depth in terms of its content.

3. You can print out the pages, "Elements of a Good Progressive Christian Worship Song" and make a hand out of this if you like. Do the songs you use in worship match up well with this list? Is there anything important that might be missing from it? If so, please point out what you think might be missing and discuss it.

4. What are some of the songs in the praise and worship music world that you like best and that you feel work well in more progressive church contexts?

SECTION THREE

~~~~~~

*The Bible and More About
Progressive Theology*

CHAPTER 11

A Progressive Approach to the Bible

A QUICK ATTEMPT TO MAKE THIS ALL VERY SIMPLE!

This chapter and the one that follows it will probably be the most challenging chapters of this book for many readers. This is why I have saved them for this final section. These chapters are really just for those of you who *want* to go deeper.

This particular chapter will focus on how progressive Christians tend to work with the Bible, and then in chapter twelve we'll get more deeply into how and why many progressive Christians no longer believe that Jesus *had* to be punished on the cross in order for God to forgive our sins.

As you'll see, these are not easy topics to explore. I'm concerned that I'll lose some of you readers because these subjects so easily get complex, controversial, intellectually demanding, and potentially confusing. So let me just sum everything up as simply as I can right now so you'll have a good sense of what this chapter on Scripture is all about even before we begin.

When all is said and done, the biggest difference between progressive Christians and others when it comes to the Bible and to doctrines like penal substitutionary atonement is this; progressive Christians believe that while God speaks to us through the words written in the Bible, *God also leads us and speaks to us through what we think and feel about the words written in the Bible.*

When I write "feel" in the previous paragraph, I'm not just talking about our all-too-fragile and volatile "warm fuzzy feelings or emotions." I'm talking about what our very beings know in our "guts" or in our hearts by virtue of our hard-earned human experience.

I'll be using the word "heart" in this chapter in the way that the Scriptures use the word—to speak of the deepest part of who we are at the very core of our beings.

More conservative Christians tend to insist that what we think or experience or know in our hearts about what the "Bible says" is irrelevant. We should just accept it, submit to it, and obey it. Progressive Christians insist that disregarding what emerges within our minds and hearts as we read the Scriptures may cause us to actually miss hearing some of the deeper things that God is trying to communicate to us.

Dr. Karl Kuhn, professor of religion at Lakeland College in Sheboygan, WI put together a fantastic overview of the some of the different ways that various kinds of Christians tend to approach the "nature" and "authority" of Scripture. This overview is included at the end of this chapter so that you can make copies of it and use it along with the discussion questions if you like. He lists five different approaches by five different groups, and I should say that I am not at all clear which perspective Dr. Kuhn himself would personally embrace. I think he is very fair in his description of each category. Here is his excellent summary of a progressive Christian way of approaching the Bible.

For Progressive Christians . . .

Regarding the nature of Scripture: *Scripture is inspired by God and a faithful testimony to God, though it frequently reflects limitations of human knowledge and perspective.*

Regarding the authority of Scripture: *Christians are called to engage in thoughtful, prayerful dialogue with our scriptural traditions, one another, and the Holy Spirit in order to discern how these traditions may lead us to become more faithful followers of Jesus in our time and place.*[1]

So there you have it. This is where we're heading in this chapter.

Now let's back up and I'll attempt to explain how and why progressive Christians work with the Bible in this way. But let me just finally say that this chapter could easily be an entire book! There's plenty that I'd love to share with you regarding a more progressive approach to Scripture that would just be too much for this project. I hope and pray I've faithfully boiled things down and covered some of the most important points.

PROGRESSIVE CHRISTIANS AND THE BIBLE

Progressive Christians do not consider the Bible to be a "magic" book. It did not somehow appear in leather bound King James Version just as we have it today. And for those of you who have a high view of Scripture I know this may sound offensive at first, but progressive Christians do not consider the Bible to be a perfect or error-free book.

Don't misunderstand me. We believe God speaks to us through Scripture in very powerful and unique and "inspired" ways, but we also believe that the Bible came into being through thoroughly human and at times imperfect processes. We do not consider it to be "God's Word" in a magical sense—as though each word was literally dictated by God and flawlessly written down by the authors of the biblical books.

HEARING THE WORD

One of the more helpful articulations of the way many progressive Christians approach Scripture is expressed in a wonderful book called Take This Bread, by Sara Miles.[2] Sarah quotes one of her pastors, a man named Donald;

> 'The Bible,' I'd heard Donald preach, isn't the Word of God. 'The Word of God,' he said, 'is what's heard by the people of God when the Bible is read.'

That meant the Word was living not because it was magical but because over and over, down the centuries, believers wrestled with texts, adapted them, edited them, interpreted them, swallowed them whole, and spat them out. The stories in the Bible were records of human attempts to understand God—attempts that were hopelessly incomplete. But, through words and acts, we kept trying. (p.173).

What a powerful statement.

"The Word of God is what's heard by the people of God when the Bible is read."

Progressive Christians tend to agree that *hearing* the Word of God through the Bible is at least a two-fold process. First, we read and listen to the literal words of the text. But second, we also listen to what we "hear" within ourselves (as individuals and in community) as we take in or absorb the portion of Scripture being read.

To put this another way, we first do our best to understand what the words of the Bible were saying to the community to which they were originally written. We read and "listen" to the words at face value. But then, we also listen to and wrestle with what comes up within our own minds and hearts as we try to understand the words in our own present time and context.

If our entire beings resonate with a portion of Scripture and we immediately respond with a deep "yes" to what a biblical text is saying, we embrace it and do our best to live it out. Pretty simple.

But, and here's where things start to get potentially controversial or complex, *we also listen to our own questions and reactions.*

If something in the Bible disturbs us greatly or somehow seems profoundly out of sync with our own deepest sense of "knowing," or if a biblical text seems to be saying something that is in stark contrast with who we understand and experience God to be, we acknowledge this and discuss it. We do our best to see if some of the tension we might be feeling is due to our own limited understanding—and this is often the case! It's totally possible that we might be missing something important. Maybe we're being stubborn. Perhaps we need to simply "submit" to a certain truth even though it initially seems shocking or difficult or somehow "cuts against our grain."

Jesus' teachings were often strange or offensive to his original listeners, and they can certainly strike us that way today. This doesn't mean that there is necessarily anything wrong with Jesus' teachings! It just might be an indication of how far away our own conventional wisdom and cultural norms have taken us from biblical Truth.

But progressive Christians also try to be open to the possibility that the Holy Spirit is actually the One who is "disturbing us" and leading us to ask some of the questions we are feeling led to ask. We try to be open to *the possibility that God's Spirit is the source of our discomfort* with what a biblical text seems to be saying at first reading or at face value. And then, as Sara Miles put it, we prayerfully and with great humility "wrestle with the text."

We work with more recently discovered sociological and/or scientific insights that may shed new light on the passage of Scripture. We take in the insights of scholars who have done extensive work on the text at hand. And then again, we pay attention to our own emotional, spiritual, and theological reactions to what the words of the Bible seem to be saying, believing that God's Spirit is *within us* and *guiding us* as we do. We believe that all of these things can be part of the process through which the Spirit whispers messages from God to us as we read the Bible.

We do these things on our own, and we do these things in community.

Acknowledging Our "Lenses"

It's not that progressive Christians are taking reckless license or liberty to "make the Bible say (or not say!) what *we* want it to say." But let's face it. We can all do exactly this if we're not extremely careful, and most of us have been guilty of reading things into the Scriptures from time to time. Progressive Christians acknowledge the simple fact that we *all* bring a huge amount of baggage with us to the reading of any text. This may be especially true when it comes to biblical texts.

The best we can hope to do is be ruthlessly honest with ourselves when it comes to the biases and issues and predispositions we bring with us as we attempt to hear God's Word through the Bible and live out our faith. These biases are like lenses that can color what we see or comprehend as we read Scripture.

As Richard Rohr insists,

> *After almost forty years of teaching and preaching, I can say: You see the text through your available eyes. You hear a text from your own level of development and consciousness. Punitive people love punitive texts; loving people hear in the same text calls to discernment, clarity, choice, and decision.*
>
> *. . . We do not see things as they are; we see things as we are. Take that as nearly certain.* (The Naked Now, p.82).[3]

Progressive Christians are not trying to manipulate the Bible. We *want* the content of biblical verses to be free and able to challenge us and redirect our thinking and living when we're somehow off track according to what we sense God is saying to us through the Scriptures.

If we are bringing a "liberal bias" or something like that to a text, we want to be aware of this and challenge ourselves not to hear a verse of Scripture a certain way simply because that's what we *want* it to say. And we'd encourage more conservative Christians to ask themselves similar questions.

On the other hand, and this is really important, we also believe that God's Holy Spirit may actually be *providing some fresh lenses that we need*—fresh insight or information or wisdom born from experience—in order to read a text more clearly, and in order to discern God's Word through the Bible more accurately.

To put this yet another way, progressive Christians contend that it's crucial to listen to what may well be our own *God-given reactions, thoughts, and insights* as we <u>dialogue</u> with the words of the Book. If, after doing the hard work of honestly asking ourselves whether or not our own biases are preventing us from "hearing God's Word," we *still* have serious questions or problems with what a portion of Scripture seems to be presenting as Divine Truth, we open ourselves to the possibility that God's Spirit is inspiring these questions of ours and leading us to search even more deeply.

And this is where a more progressive way of reading Scripture may seem very different and perhaps dangerous to those who take a more "literalist" approach to the Bible. In its extreme form, a literalist approach is summed up in bumper sticker statements such as,

"The Bible says it. I believe it. That settles it."

Progressive Christians don't tend to boil things down very easily to bumper sticker statements! But if we did, our Bible bumper sticker might say something more like,

"Faithful but imperfect human beings wrote the Scriptures. God was with them and guiding them as they did. We study what they wrote, question it, react to it, and critique and clarify it in Spirit-led community so that we can understand what God is saying to us today through the text. It's never simply settled, because God is always opening up new insights to us and shedding new light on what the Scriptures do and do not mean."

Something like that.

Yeah, it would have to be a big bumper!

I realize that this more progressive way of reading scripture can be tricky stuff. It requires a great deal of honesty, humility, spiritual maturity, and sometimes additional work to read the Bible this way. It goes without saying that a lot of people just don't want to have to put that much effort into reading Scripture, and the literalist approach is in many ways simpler and less time consuming. I understand that. But the stakes are high.

One of the things I often say to people about the Bible is that "it's an easy book to misinterpret, a difficult book to read well, but worth the trouble."

It's worth the trouble because there are times, in my opinion, when the more progressive approach to Scripture which I'm trying to share with you here will enable us to hear and respond to God's Word through the Bible *more deeply and more faithfully.*

Yes, there are risks that this more progressive approach to Scripture might cause us to read things into biblical texts that God never intended, or that it might prevent us from receiving a difficult biblical truth which God really does want us to hear and honor. But I would suggest that the very same dangers exist when we take a literalist approach to the Bible.

A literalist reading of Scripture could cause us to read things as "biblical truth" that God never intended, or that God may have intended for a specific historical context—but not for all time and all contexts.

This is especially true when it comes to some of the difficult issues that have caused huge divisions in the Church historically (slavery, "manifest destiny," gender roles, ordination of women, the death penalty, same gender sexuality, etc).

God's Word In The Bible *AND* In Human Eyes

I want to share a quick story that has often haunted me (in a good way) when it comes to reading the Bible. It is from Henri Nouwen's wonderful little book called <u>Wounded Healer.</u>[4]

> *One day a young fugitive, trying to hide himself from the enemy, entered a small village. The people were kind to him and offered him a place to stay. But when the soldiers who sought the fugitive asked where he was hiding, everyone became very fearful. The soldiers threatened to burn the village and kill every man in it unless the young man was handed over to them before dawn.*

The people went to the minister and asked him what to do. The minister, torn between handing over the boy to the enemy or having his people killed, withdrew to his room and read his Bible, hoping to find an answer before dawn. After many hours, in the early morning his eyes fell on these words;

'It is better that one man dies than that the whole people be lost.'

Then the minister closed the Bible, called the soldiers and told them where the boy was hidden. And after the soldiers led the fugitive away to be killed, there was a feast in the village because the minister had saved the lives of the people. But the minister did not celebrate. Overcome with a deep sadness, he remained in his room.

That night an angel came to him, and asked, 'What have you done?'

He said: 'I handed over the fugitive to the enemy.'

Then the angel said, 'But don't you know that you handed over the Messiah?'

'How could I know?' the minister replied anxiously.

Then the angel said: 'If, instead of reading your Bible, you had visited this young man just once and looked into his eyes, you would have known.'

That last line nails me every time. There are so many times when I find myself wanting to say to a Christian friend who is arguing what he or she considers to be a biblically based point of view (usually regarding some social issue like same gender sexuality)—"Put down the Bible for a minute and look into the eyes of one of the people you are talking about—get to know the person as a human being—his or her story, pain, what makes him or her laugh and cry—and you might think and feel differently about what you are claiming 'the Bible says' regarding this person or this issue."

Again, the point is that reading Scripture deeply and faithfully is more than just reading the literal words of the text. It's about honoring the Words

God speaks as we *both* read the text *and* listen for what can sometimes only be "heard" as we look into the eyes of another human being.

As feminist theologians have been reminding us for decades now, we need to honor and listen to the divinely incarnate Word of God *in our own human experience* as we also honor and listen to the literal words of the Book. And, if and when something in the Bible strikes us to be in stark contrast with what our own hearts and minds somehow *know deep down in our spirits* to be true (or not true), we are not honoring God by setting aside what our own experience and living has taught us. In fact, most progressive Christians would insist that it is unwise, unfaithful, and potentially catastrophic to disregard what our own hearts know.

I want to acknowledge that I'm very familiar with most of the strong and very sincere evangelical responses at this point. I've had this conversation many times over the years, and I realize that it can sound rebellious or arrogant for us to suggest that we need to trust and honor what our own human hearts tell us to be true. The Scriptures themselves warn us against our own capacity for self-deception;

"God's ways are not our ways (Isaiah 55:8)." "There is a way which seems right to a man (sic), but the end thereof is death (Proverbs 14:12)." "The human heart is deceitful above all things. (Jeremiah 17:9)." "Lean not on your own understanding. (Proverbs 3:4)."

Believe me, all of these verses and several others are very much before me as I write this chapter. But as I've stated, progressive Christians are insisting that there is greater potential danger and damage to be done in the name of religion when we ignore or disregard our honest human reactions and "knowing" altogether.

As Richard Rohr once put it in a speaking engagement (which I cite here from memory),

One of the most unfortunate things the Church did to many people historically was to make it almost impossible for us to trust our own experience. We need to be encouraged to trust what we know to be true or not true, because so often that is how God is speaking to us.[5]

Yes, our "experience" can be wrong. Sometimes tragically so. I love the old saying of Will Rogers,

It's not what we know that hurts; it's what we know that ain't so![6]

But it's precisely because we *can* be wrong, even when it comes to positions we hold passionately, that we need to do our wrestling and questioning of Scripture together with other people who also love God, who don't always agree with us, and who can challenge us and keep us honest and open.

But if and when something that "the Bible says" at face value or first reading seems to be in great tension with *what we know through our own experience to somehow be or not be true*, progressive Christians have learned to be open to the possibility that what the Bible seems to be saying may actually be out of sync with the very will and character and intentions of God.

Again, I realize how scary and presumptuous and dangerous this can all sound to some of us, so in a moment I'll give an example of how this more progressive approach to Scripture worked itself out in a very well known historical situation.

BEYOND "PROOF-TEXTING"

But before we move to our concrete example, we need to take a quick look at one more important issue when it comes to a progressive approach to the Bible. We need to understand the danger of what is often referred to as "proof-texting."

Basically, proof-texting is the practice of lifting out certain isolated verses from Scripture, removing them from their original historical and cultural context and their place in the overall witness of the Bible, and then building opinions or sometimes entire doctrines around these isolated verses.

Proof-texting is dangerous because it can be used to make the Bible justify all kinds of extreme things if we're not careful. If we isolate a single verse, take it out of context and argue that "this is what the Bible says," then all kinds of crazy things can be presented as being "biblically based." For example, Deuteronomy 21:18-21 instructs parents to kill a son or daughter who is rebellious. Strict obedience to such a law without understanding it in light of the overall message of the Bible would be disastrous!

So in addition to working with our own questions, biases, insights, and experience as we read Scripture, progressive Christians also do our best to be aware of the limitations and dangers of proof-texting—of building opinions and doctrines around individual texts that are lifted out of the overall message of the Bible. If and when there are certain portions of Scripture which seem, after prayerful exploration, to be in great tension with the entire witness of the Bible, we let the overall witness be our guide and thus our authority.

You might say that we actually "use the *whole* Bible to critique *isolated portions* of the Bible."

Okay. I imagine that some of you are thoroughly confused by now! I hope I haven't given you a migraine. I understand that this is all pretty heady stuff. So let's get out of the theoretical realm and I'll show you an example of how this more progressive way of reading Scripture actually worked in real life regarding a very controversial and hugely important issue. I'm referring to how the Church dealt with the Bible when it came to the issue of slavery.

THE EXAMPLE OF THE BIBLE AND SLAVERY

It's not hard at all to isolate certain verses from the Bible and use these verses to argue that the institution of slavery is biblically grounded and permissible. Sadly, history points out that many well intentioned (and some not so much!) slave holding Christians did precisely this. They'd point to Colossians 3:22, for example, which literally says, "Slaves, obey your masters." They'd point out that Jesus never directly critiqued the institution of slavery, and that he even used the metaphor of the slave/master relationship several times in his teachings. They'd highlight that the apostle Paul required Onesimus, an escaped slave, to return to his master (Philemon 18ff). There are plenty more verses that were used in this way. So you see, a case could easily be made that the Bible actually sanctions slavery.

But what happened was that increasing numbers of Christians eventually determined that while individual Bible verses could be interpreted as indicating that God had no problem with slavery, *the overall witness of Scripture suggested otherwise.*

They realized that when you read the entire Bible, you get the sense of a God who promotes freedom, who is about justice, and who takes the side of the oppressed, the poor, the downtrodden, and the outcast. You read about the God who "heard the cries of God's people" when they were slaves in Egypt and who liberated them and called them to be a Light to the nations. You read about Jesus summing up all the laws and the prophets with teachings such as "Love your neighbor as yourself," and "treat others as you yourself would like to be treated."

So on the basis of this broader picture of the character and heart and will of God throughout the entire Bible, and on the basis of what their own hearts and consciences *knew to be right and wrong,* Christians began to stand against slavery and for universal human freedom—even though they sometimes *appeared* or *seemed* to be actually disregarding those biblical verses that were isolated and used to endorse slavery.

Does this make sense to you? I hope so.

As I've now written many times throughout this book, you don't need to agree with anything I've written. I'm not trying to convince you to think as a progressive Christian might, or to read Scripture as progressive Christians do.

But I want you to understand that it's neither accurate nor fair to conclude that progressive Christians "aren't biblical." We're very biblical, but just in a different way than many other Christians.

Having laid this foundation, let's move on now to some of the theological issues that were alluded to under the third Mark of Progressive Christian Worship Music. Yes, all of this *is* relevant to what this book is actually about!

THE FUNCTION OF SCRIPTURE
IN CHRISTIAN TRADITION

By Karl Kuhn, Professor of Religion at Lakeland College in Sheboygan, WI; used with permission

The Nature and Authority of Sacred Scripture

Nature:　　how, exactly, Scripture came to be, and its resulting character

Authority:　how Scripture is to serve as a source of Christian thought and practice

Extraordinary Diversity of Perspectives: Despite the incredible significance of Scripture in Christian tradition, Christian theologians embrace a dizzying array of perspectives on the nature and authority of Scripture.

Fundamentalist:

Nature:　　Scripture is the inerrant Word of God, fully truthful on all matters it addresses.

Authority:　Christians are bound to embrace all that Scripture speaks on matters of science, history, doctrine and practice.

Conservative:

Nature:　　Scripture is the infallible Word of God, though it may use approximations in the reporting of events and reflect scientific knowledge/standards of the time.

Authority:　Christians are bound to embrace all that Scripture dictates on matters of science and history (with some qualification), and all that Scripture speaks on matters of doctrine and practice.

Moderate:

Nature:　　Scripture is inspired by God, though it may occasionally reflect limitations of human knowledge and cultural perspectives.

Authority:　Unless certain teachings are known to conflict with science and historiography, or are heavily conditioned by the cultural context of the writers, Scripture is to be embraced as a normative guide for Christian thoughts and practice, as discerned through careful interpretation, dialogue and prayer.

Progressive:

Nature: Scripture is inspired by God and a faithful testimony to God, though it frequently reflects limitations of human knowledge and perspective.

Authority: Christians are called to engage in thoughtful, prayerful dialogue with our scriptural traditions, one another, and the Holy Spirit in order to discern how these traditions may lead us to become more faithful followers of Jesus in our time and place.

Revisionist:

Nature: Scripture is no more inspired than other religious works, and should not function as a *uniquely normative* guide for religious thought and practice.

Authority: It should be held in dialogue with other religious and philosophical traditions.

Chapter 11: Questions For Discussion

1. Share a bit about your "relationship" with the Bible. Do you read it often? Is it vital and alive for you? It is too confusing or difficult to read to be helpful to you?

2. Why is the Bible so important to us as Christians—and especially to Protestant Christians in light of what the Reformation was all about?

3. Which of the five different perspectives Dr. Karl Kuhn summarized do you find yourself most in agreement with at this point in your spiritual journey?

4. Do you think the Bible is a "perfect book?" Does it need to be "perfect" in order for God to speak through it to us in authoritative and transforming ways?

5. What do you think about Sara Mile's pastor's remark that "The Word of God is what is heard by the people of God when the Bible is read"?

6. What are the pro's and con's of listening to our own thoughts, questions, and reactions to what the Bible is saying or *seems* to be saying?

7. Have you ever disregarded what your own heart felt or knew to be true (or not true) in order to submit to a biblical teaching? Was this a wise and necessary thing to do? Have you changed your way of looking at this teaching at all?

8. Does anything about this chapter cause you to be uncomfortable? Do you find this way of approaching the Bible to be helpful?

9. Close with a prayer that God's Holy Spirit will help you and your congregation to hear God's Word through Scripture as clearly, accurately, and responsibly as possible. Pray that your music ministry will reflect biblical Truth with integrity and clarity.

CHAPTER 12

More About Progressive Theology

As was stated in the third chapter, "Progressive Theology" is the most difficult of the 6 Marks for me to try to explain. Because some of the issues opened up in that chapter are too important and potentially controversial to touch upon superficially, I feel as though I owe those of you who really care about these topics (and about me) some additional elaboration. So that's what this chapter is about.

That being said, I'm still concerned that this chapter is going to be too much for some readers. My apologies in advance if this kind of deeper theological reflection is a bit overwhelming.

At the same time, a big part of what this book is all about is an invitation and a challenge to musicians in churches to become more serious musical theologians—which simply means to think more deeply about how God, the Bible, and your Christian faith is connected to the music and lyrics you bring into worship. I know you are totally capable of taking on this challenge, and the truth is that the Church at this point in history really *needs* its' musicians to become better theologians. As someone once put it (I can't recall where I heard this), "We need our artists to become better theologians, and we need our theologians to become better artists."

As you'll see, each of the ideas and topics we're about to touch upon here could easily be the focus of an entire manuscript. Even with this additional chapter I'm going to acknowledge from the outset that my reflections are going to be incomplete and inadequate in many ways. There are nuances and tangents I'd love to explore even more fully, but it would just be too much.

I also want to acknowledge that some of the ideas expressed in this chapter will probably be new and at the very least a "stretch" for some readers. If you've grown up steeped in more conservative or traditional understandings of what the Christian faith is about, you may even wind up feeling as though I and other progressive Christians have totally lost our way. I guess all I can ask is that you try to read this chapter with an open mind and heart, read it all the way through, and feel free to contact me if you have serious questions or concerns you'd like to address or discuss in more detail.

I also want you to know how much respect I have for the faith of those of you who are reading this, and for the issues we're going to explore in this chapter. I have no desire to confuse you or to in any way undermine the understanding of the Bible and Christianity you cherish and that may have literally saved your life and opened up God's love and truth to you. You do not need to agree with anything written here. I'm simply trying to help you understand how and why many progressive Christians are questioning certain traditional doctrines and understandings of biblical faith at this point in history.

So part of what I'm saying in this preface full of qualifiers is—you don't have to read this chapter! It's kind of long and heavy at times, and if you already read the first two sections of this book then you have gotten the heart and soul of what this entire work is about.

Of course I hope you do read on.

But I don't want you to over-think your faith in ways that are not helpful to you. There's a Zen saying, attributed to anonymous monks, that simply says,

> *Do not plunder the Mystery with concepts.*

I'm probably in danger of doing a bit of "Mystery plundering" in this chapter, so by all means separate the wheat from the chaff as God's Spirit leads you.

And finally, before we get into this chapter, please also understand that I myself am always in process theologically. My beliefs, convictions, interpretations of Scripture, and viewpoints on doctrines have evolved so much over the years that I now hold these things with a great deal of humility and openness of mind and heart. As I said, if anything you read here causes you confusion or concern, please feel free to contact me, share your thoughts, and push back against what I'm saying if you need to (hopefully with kindness and respect!). Let's see how we can help each other discern God's Truth with as much integrity as possible—even when we might ultimately need to agree to disagree.

THE HOT TOPIC—PENAL SUBSTITUTIONARY ATONEMENT

Okay let's get down to work. As I mentioned in Chapter Three, most progressive Christians are at the very least seriously questioning the doctrine of penal substitutionary atonement (PSA). Many progressive Christians have flat out rejected this doctrine, and some with downright evangelical fervor! So let's take a moment to get clear on what the doctrine of penal substitutionary atonement is. Then I'll attempt to explain how and why many progressive Christians are turning away from this doctrine while at the same time still remaining passionately Christian.

According to the doctrine of PSA, sin entered the world when Adam and Eve disobeyed God in the Garden of Eden. From that point forward, according to this doctrine, all humans have been "born into sin" and are hopelessly "sinful by nature." As one preacher recently joked, "it's kind of like sin in this sense is a sexually transmitted disease"[1]. We "catch" or inherit our sinful nature from our sinful biological parents, who caught it from their parents, and it goes all the way back to Adam and Eve. There's nothing we can do to prevent this. There's no way any human can ever be "good enough" to be cured from this sin disease or to earn his or her way into God's favor and eternal acceptance.

According to this doctrine, God is holy and perfect, and the only way a perfectly holy God can accept sinful human beings into God's presence (Heaven) is for someone to pay the full price for the sins that Adam and

Eve committed and that all humans have committed since Adam and Eve. Someone or something has to first be punished in order to pay the penalty for all of this sin and to satisfy the legal requirements of God's "justice." Only then can God forgive our transgressions and open up the perfect realm of Heaven to us.

So God provided the only possible cure for this "sin disease." God sent God's own son, Jesus, to become the perfect sacrifice for human sins. Jesus became the perfect blood sacrifice—in accordance with the Hebrew laws in Scripture—and he "atoned" for the sins of humankind by taking our punishment onto himself. The sins of the people were "put on" innocent Jesus—the ultimate sacrificial lamb "without spot or blemish." On the cross, Jesus paid the price for our sins, and all we need to do is believe this in our hearts and confess it with our lips and God will then "impute" to us the righteousness of Jesus.

Forgiven by God through the sacrifice of Jesus, our sins are washed away by Christ's blood, and we are made acceptable to God for eternity. That's the "good news."

But if we do not "receive Christ" in this way and believe that he died for us on the cross so that our sinful nature and our sinful acts can be forgiven, then we remain sinful and therefore unacceptable to God. The punishment for our sin is to be tortured in the fires of hell for all eternity with no possibility of escape. All humans who are not Christians in this way—all persons of other religions who do not "confess Jesus" in this way—are headed for everlasting hellfire.

As I wrote in the third chapter, most progressive Christians do not embrace this doctrine because we do not believe it accurately reflects the amazing grace and unconditional love of God. This doctrine, according to progressive Christians, makes God out to be some kind of ruthless tyrant. "Believe this or I (God) will see to it that you are tortured forever!" Most progressive Christians contend that this doctrine just doesn't jive with the heart of God that is revealed throughout the entire Bible and in our own human experience.

But here's the problem.

It's not that Christians who believe in this doctrine are all mean, judgmental, unmerciful people. Some might be, but that's beside the point. And for that matter, there are plenty of mean, self-righteous, judgmental progressive Christians in the world as well (they/we just tend to judge conservative Christians or those who don't recycle or those who disagree with us in one way or another!).

But the problem is that there are plenty of verses in the Bible that can be read to support the doctrine of penal substitutionary atonement. Proponents of PSA argue that they didn't just make this stuff up out of thin air. They believe that this is what the Bible actually tells us, and they can point to many verses in Scripture that lead them to embrace this doctrine.

So, as was mentioned in the previous chapter, defenders of PSA will often respond to the positions of progressive Christians by saying things like, "Look—it doesn't ultimately matter what 'rings true to you,' or what 'your own human experience has taught you' about how loving God is. It doesn't matter what you think or feel about the notion of blood sacrifice or God punishing people or sending them to hell—that's what the Bible says and we believe the Bible is God's Word and the ultimate authority for our faith."

And this is why I devoted the entire previous chapter to "a progressive way of approaching the Bible." If you read that chapter, then I trust you can imagine what a progressive Christian's response to the previous paragraph might be. We would say that it really *does matter* what we think and feel about what the Bible says, and that God's Spirit might actually be leading us and guiding us through our thoughts and feelings to question certain things that are in the Scriptures. We would say that God is still speaking to us, shedding fresh light upon biblical texts, and inviting us to honor our own deepest "knowing," in community with others, as we listen for God's messages to us.

THE PROBLEMS WITH BLOOD SACRIFICE AND PENAL SUBSTITUTIONARY ATONEMENT

Despite its obvious prevalence in the Bible, increasing numbers of progressive Christians wonder if it was truly God's intention for blood sacrifice to have ever had such a central role in Jewish and Christian spirituality, Scripture, and ritual.

Now I know that may be a mind blowing statement to some of you. I'm well aware of verses such as Hebrews 9:22—"Without the shedding of blood there can be no forgiveness of sins." I'm well aware of the central place that "the blood of Jesus" plays in the theology of most of evangelical Christianity, and in many cherished hymns such as "Nothing But The Blood of Jesus." I get this, and I have deep respect for the role and power of this theology in many people's lives.

But what's increasingly going on in progressive Christian circles is that many folks are finally admitting to themselves and others that there is something about this whole blood sacrifice thing—the ritualized shedding of the blood of innocent animals in Judaism and the sacrifice of animals and human children in other religions—that just doesn't make sense or feel True or even healthy to us. Something in our hearts is telling us that this emphasis on ritualized violence against an innocent victim in order to "appease God" is just plain off.

In other words, even though there is plenty about blood sacrifice in the Bible, many progressive Christians are now questioning the biblical grounding of the institution of blood sacrifice in the same way that Christians questioned the biblical grounding of the institution of slavery. We're listening to what we trust is the voice of God within our own hearts as we also listen to the overall witness of the entire Bible.

LET'S GET TO THE POINT

No one really knows where the practice of animal or human blood sacrifice originated. The Hebrews were certainly not the first or the only people to practice this way of trying to placate or appease the wrath of a demanding and judgmental Divinity. No one can say for sure how or why this "scapegoat mechanism" came to dominate the religious understanding of the Hebrew people in the ways it obviously did. I'm not an authority on this topic, and I'm also guessing that not too many readers of this book are feeling the need for deep exploration of the origins of blood sacrifice.

I suggest the work of scholar Rene Girard however to those of you who might indeed be interested in a serious academic exploration of how the practice of animal sacrifice "worked" psychologically for a tribal people. If you don't want to read Girard's rather academic and somewhat complex work on the subject, his main points are brilliantly summed up by blogger, theologian, and author Tony Jones in his excellent new book, <u>A Better Atonement</u>.[2] I highly recommend this book and I'll be drawing from it again shortly.

But here's the point for our purposes.

Many progressive Christians no longer believe that Jesus *had* to be killed and his blood "offered" so that God could forgive and fully accept sinful humans into God's presence. As mentioned briefly in the third chapter, increasing numbers of people are acknowledging that this way of understanding the cross of Jesus makes God seem ruthless and small minded and even petty. It violates what our hearts and our experience and the overall witness of the Bible has taught us about the loving character of God. It makes God a practitioner of human sacrifice. It makes God seem like someone in need of anger management therapy. It makes God seem abusive. Who is this God who would demand that His own son be tortured and put to death in order to be willing to forgive others? What kind of God would consign people to never-ending agony simply because they don't believe the right stuff or because someone else ate a piece of forbidden fruit? We wouldn't dream of doing this to our own children. Is God less loving than we are? All of this just doesn't feel consistent with the loving, merciful, gracious Being whom the entire biblical narrative reveals God to be.

Yes, it is more palatable to focus on the Incarnation when it comes to the death of Jesus. That is, if we focus on seeing Jesus as "God in human form," then instead of God (or Satan—who ultimately is subject to God's authority) requiring the death of God's own son in order to forgive us, it's a matter of God laying down His or Her own life in the person of Jesus in order to pay the price for our sins. At least in this way of understanding things God in a sense puts the price for sin "on God's own tab."

But even this approach to the cross depicts God as one who requires and demands that someone or something must be punished—even if that someone is God's own self. And that's what many progressive Christians find most troublesome—the notion of a God who *demands punishment*—a "pound of flesh"—in order for forgiveness to be possible.

I know, those last three paragraphs were awfully thick. You might need to read them a few times.

I did . . .

And I know it's scary and it sounds potentially arrogant and rebellious to even give voice to such questions. For many people the message that Jesus had to be crucified in order to satisfy God's "justice" and to make us acceptable to God here on earth and in the life to come is the essence of the Gospel itself.

Questioning this doctrine also flies against the extent to which so many of us have been taught *not* to trust our own "human ways of thinking." As I wrote in the previous chapter on a progressive approach to Scripture, I'm very familiar with the biblical warnings regarding our own capacity for self-deception and the potential limitations of our own wisdom. To quote those texts again, "God's ways are not our ways (Isaiah 55:8)." "There is a way which seems right to a man (sic), but the end thereof is death (Proverbs 14:12)." "The human heart is deceitful above all things (Jeremiah 17:9)." "Lean not on your own understanding (Proverbs 3:4)."

As I've often shared with people, I've been humbled and amazed by my own capacity to be flat out wrong at times. I've had some blind spots and errors in my life that in retrospect were really quite impressive—especially when I remember that at the time I was totally convinced I was right and that my opinions would never change! This is why I hold just about everything—including what I'm writing in this chapter—with an open mind and heart and hand. And this is why I always seek the wise counsel of groups of people whom I trust and who love God enough to challenge me and hold me accountable.

And yet, as was also stated in the last chapter, it is extremely dangerous for us to disregard our own deepest sense of knowing. God's Holy Spirit is within us. If our hearts and minds are open, humble, biblically informed and educated, and full of love for God and for God's truth beyond all else, then we *dare not* silence or disregard what God's Spirit in our very beings is saying to us through our own minds and hearts.

DIFFERENT WAYS OF UNDERSTANDING THE DEATH OF JESUS

In A Better Atonement, Tony Jones helps us to understand that Church doctrines—even doctrines as pervasive and deeply rooted as "Original Sin" and penal substitutionary atonement—were created and established by human beings who lived in particular contexts, had their own biases, and who often developed their positions in response to specific historical circumstances.

The doctrine of original sin for example—the idea that all humans are "born into sin"—that all human beings genetically inherit sin and deserve eternal damnation because of the transgression of Adam and Eve in the Garden of Eden—was not embraced fully or widely by the Church until Augustine of Hippo formulated his version of it in the 4th century. It is one possible way of making sense of what happened as a result of the man and woman eating the forbidden fruit in the Garden, but it is not the only way. Christians did just fine without this doctrine for close to four hundred years.

Most scholars agree that the doctrine of penal substitutionary atonement as we know it was not developed until 1098 when it was articulated by St. Anselm. According to Tony Jones,

> *While some might argue otherwise, penal substitutionary atonement was unknown before its development by Anselm of Canterbury in his 1098*

book, Cur Deus Homo (Why a God-Man?). Therein, Anselm introduced the first substitutionary explanation of the atonement.[3]

Anselm's expression of PSA was his response to the "problem" raised by Augustine's doctrine of Original Sin. The Eastern Orthodox tradition, which split from the Western Church in the late 11th century, did not embrace the doctrine of Original Sin at all, and so there are many Christians throughout the world who have never believed in either of these doctrines.

The key point here is that doctrines are human inventions. Centuries of devoted Christians did just fine before Augustine and Anselm came up with their positions. Doctrines are not "objective truth." They are not "simply what the Bible says." They are potential ways of understanding the biblical message, put together by people. Faithful people in most cases. Leaders of the Church. But certainly not infallible (no offense Roman Catholic brothers and sisters!). Doctrines evolve. They ebb and flow over time. They can be changed or corrected or even deemed heretical.

Again, I don't want to get into too much detail that won't serve our purposes here. So here's the point.

A doctrine such as PSA is at best one possible way among many of trying to understand what the Bible says to us, of trying to resolve the dilemma posed by the doctrine of Original Sin (how God deals with the sin that St. Augustine insisted we've inherited from Adam and Eve), and of understanding the meaning of Jesus' death on the cross. But there is no one "correct biblical way" to understand these things.

I know this is hard for many of us to accept, because we have been taught that things like Original Sin and PSA are what the Bible says, period. But that's not the case. They are *possible* ways of *interpreting* what the Bible says. But they are not the only way.

In fact, there are at least five *other* ways in which the Church over the past two thousand years has attempted to come to terms with the meaning of Jesus' crucifixion. They are *all* based on interpretations of Scripture. I'll list them here, but you'll have to do your own research and/or read <u>A</u>

Better Atonement if you'd like to know more about each of them. Here are five additional theories of the atonement that are mentioned by Tony Jones;

1. Union with God (Jesus' death unites us with God)
2. Ransom Captive (Jesus' death pays off a debt; not a punishment)
3. Cristus Victor (Jesus' death defeats the powers of sin and death)
4. Moral Exemplar (Jesus' life is our example; he was killed because he represented a challenge to the powers that be)
5. The Last Scapegoat (Jesus' death was to *end* the system of blood sacrifice)

Tony Jones suggests that there is no need for us to choose one theory of the atonement over others. He quotes author Scot Mcknight who argues that we can learn about all of these doctrines and use them like ". . . clubs in a golfer's bag. None is superior to the rest; each is appropriate for a different circumstance."[4]

WHERE I AM WITH JESUS' DEATH AND THE MEANING OF THE CROSS

As I write these words, I'm a few days away from my 54th birthday. I first heard Jesus' call to "follow me" when I was 17 years old. So I've been at this Christian discipleship thing for a while now. Interestingly, as the years go by, I find that I'm less and less focused on the whole area of "atonement" in general, and I find myself less and less concerned with "believing the right stuff" in order to avoid God's anger or wrath.

But please don't get me wrong. I'm not trying to be flip, irreverent, biblically irresponsible, theologically sloppy, or disrespectful of concerns regarding what it takes to "be right" with God. When I say that I'm less focused on atonement, I'm not saying that I don't care about the subject. I care more than ever to help people understand that they are never truly separated from God unless they somehow choose to try to ignore God's presence and love for them. But even then the Divine is always reaching out with love and trying to get through to us. I'm more into following Jesus and to trying to spread the Gospel than ever. I love God and the

Christ revealed in and through Jesus more each day. I have tremendous respect and affection for the Bible (some who know me best sometimes call me a "Bible nerd"), and I'm more blown away than ever by the depth and beauty of God's love for me and for all humankind and for Creation.

But as time goes by, I'm convinced that God's Grace is even more all-encompassing and radical than most of us will dare to allow ourselves to believe. In other words, I'm less concerned with what it takes to "be right with God" because I'm more convinced that it's virtually impossible to "be wrong with God." That doesn't mean that our lives are necessarily in alignment with God's will or purposes or God's dream for our individual lives and the well-being of the universe. We may be radically and tragically lost or alienated from our true selves and engaged in all kinds of horrible patterns and behaviors and systems that break God's heart and bring unimaginable suffering into our lives, into the lives of others, and into this world.

But I think the Bible and our own open hearts reveal to us a God who is just plain crazy in love with all of us—much the way healthy parents are with their children—except magnified exponentially beyond anything we can imagine.

Again, to quote Richard Rohr—who obviously is one of my favorite sources of inspiration—I have a deep feeling that "the Good News is much 'gooder' than most of us can possibly accept!"[5]

I really do believe that God's Love for us is so relentless and unconditional that every human being is going to have a profoundly beautiful surprise when life in these bodies of ours reaches an end. That's my heart's deepest spiritually and biblically educated hunch, and while I know that many well intentioned and deeply committed Christians will disagree with me here, I'm owning this educated spiritual hunch of mine and proclaiming it more and more. People really need to know how loved we all are. That's where we find the healing and the hope and the power for personal and social transformation that we all need—in the wild and "unreasonable" love of God.

Of course I could be wrong, and if I am I trust that God will reveal my errors to me whenever the time is right. I'm open, and I'm listening. I guess I'll have to write another book if that happens! And I'm not trying to be cavalier here at all. Believe me, I'm well aware of James' words (James 3:1) about "teachers being judged with greater strictness." I have no desire at all to mislead anyone, and I take my responsibility as a teacher of Scripture and the Christian faith very seriously.

But if the Bible and my own faith journey help make anything clear, it is that God is unconditionally wild about us all. God is passionately and unconditionally in love with *you*. There's nothing to be afraid of—plenty to respect and approach with awe and great reverence—but nothing to fear. We are all "perfectly loved," and as it says in 1 John 4:18, "perfect love casts out all fear."

By the way, the Hebrew word that is often translated with the English word "fear," as in "the fear of the LORD is the beginning of wisdom" (Proverbs 9:10), could also just as legitimately be translated with the word "reverence." I have great reverence and respect for God. But I do not think God is interested in frightening us, and I certainly do not think that God has any desire to try to threaten us into a relationship.

At the same time, I do think that what we believe matters tremendously. I obviously have spent a lot of time and energy coming to terms with what I believe and why.

In light of what I've just written, it might surprise you now to know that I'm actually more traditional in many of my Christian beliefs than you might imagine, and more so than many of my progressive Christian friends. I'm able to embrace and sometimes redefine or re-imagine many traditional Christian doctrines and find profound meaning, beauty, and life-changing power in them.

THE END OF SACRIFICIAL KILLING
(THE LAST SCAPEGOAT)

For example, while I do not believe that Jesus had to be put to death in order for God to be willing to forgive us, I also do not agree with those who want to somehow simply ignore the whole reality of blood sacrifice throughout Scripture. Jesus certainly could not just ignore it. Whether our modern ears and sensibilities like it or not, the Jews were elaborately wrapped up in the practice of ritual sacrifice. It's a significant part of the biblical narrative. And, there are very important aspects of Jesus' story, such as the cleansing of the temple, that are intimately connected to the practice of animal sacrifice and some of the problems that went along with it.

This is where the doctrine which Tony Jones refers to as "The Last Scapegoat" appeals to me. It's a relatively new doctrine historically, and it's articulated very powerfully by Rene Girard. Again, read <u>A Better Atonement</u> for a really nice summary of this position.

But to state it simply, Girard suggests that Jesus may have embraced the role of "Lamb of God" in order to put a complete end to the system of blood sacrifice, and in order to end all forms of "penal substitutionary atonement." Perhaps Jesus was saying something like, "Look—this animal sacrifice thing isn't pleasing to God, it never really was, and it isn't working anyway! It stops here and now with me. Never again will anyone or anything—innocent or otherwise—be slaughtered in the Name of God! Stop this! No more of this! It ends now, here, with me."

So in that sense, I can imagine Jesus laying down his own life (as opposed to God insisting that he be sacrificed) in order to end the entire system and practice of ritual sacrifices altogether. In that light, Jesus as The Lamb of God makes beautiful sense to me. He brilliantly fulfilled all of the elaborate requirements of priestly blood sacrifices—the Lamb "without spot or blemish"—not in order to *be* the ultimate sacrifice, but to *put an end to the ritual practice of blood sacrifice* completely.

The Psychological Power of the Cross

Sometimes I think of God, the One who designed and created human beings, as an Ultimate Psychologist of sorts. Obviously the Creator knows what makes human beings tick. God knows that one of the hardest things psychologically for many of us is to *believe and accept* that we are loved unconditionally and that we are truly and fully forgiven when we screw up.

And I mean *really screw up*. God knows how excruciatingly difficult it is for many of us to be able to fully forgive ourselves for some of the things we've done. For many complex reasons, the burden of guilt and shame that countless people carry around is impossible to overstate.

Incidentally, there is a distinction between guilt and shame I've recently heard and/or read in several places that I think is helpful;

> *Guilt is feeling bad about something we've done; Shame is feeling bad about who we are.*

I like this distinction. There is good guilt which is meant to help us look at ourselves and take responsibility for choices that "miss the mark." We might call this "conviction." It's meant to get our soul's attention and point us in the right direction. But shame is another matter, and it is rarely (if ever) healthy in my opinion, and certainly should not ever be used as a disciplinary tactic—especially in the name of God.

But back to my point.

I won't take too much time to develop what I'm getting at here, but sometimes I wonder if God knew that it was going to take something very extreme and radical and "messy" for some of us to be able to *allow ourselves* to be set free from our own shame and resulting self-hatred. I've met so many people over the years who simply cannot believe that God truly loves them, and they simply cannot let themselves off the hook for things they've done and about which they feel horribly ashamed. For many such people, it is deeply powerful for them to think of the cross as an expression of just how far God is willing to go in order to show us how wildly loved we truly are.

Author Brennan Manning has influenced my thinking a good deal regarding the psychological power of the cross. He's a recovering alcoholic, and in one of his books called The Ragamuffin Gospel[6] he describes an AA intervention in which a man was present who had done something so horrible that he couldn't forgive himself. On a Christmas Eve, this man had taken his daughter out to buy a special present. He stopped at his favorite tavern on the way home at about three in the afternoon, left the motor running so the heat would be on, told his young daughter to stay in the car, and locked the doors from the outside. He went in the bar, ran into some old army buddies, and started drinking.

You guessed it. He got drunk and forgot his daughter was in the car. Hours went by. The car stalled. When he finally came out at midnight, his daughter had nearly frozen to death. Her hands and ears were so severely frostbitten that her thumb had to be amputated and her hearing was permanently damaged. They were lucky she did not freeze to death.

Once the man got out of denial and fully faced what he had done, he was beside himself with grief, shame, and self-loathing. He could not believe that anyone—including God—could or would ever forgive him, and he certainly could not forgive himself.

Brennan initially shared this story to explain the importance of getting out of denial and honestly facing the truth about ourselves and some of our actions. But then he went on to explain that it was the cross of Jesus that began to open up a way out of this man's dungeon of shame. The cross somehow proclaimed the mind-blowing truth that God loved this man—despite his unspeakable failures and catastrophic mistakes—so much that God would even take on human flesh and become a bloody mess in order to show this man (and all of us) how radical, deep, extreme, messy, and all-encompassing God's love for every human being truly is.

This enabled this broken man to begin to believe that just perhaps he was still worth being loved, even though he'd screwed up so badly that he could barely face himself or his family. If God in Jesus would literally die for him—knowing full well the truth about this man's life—then maybe there was hope for him somehow. It enabled him to begin the process of forgiving himself, or to at least believe that such forgiveness was possible.

It enabled him to take responsibility for his actions, to humbly face his family and the drastic consequences of his actions, and to begin the long journey of trying to somehow rebuild relationships and his own sense of dignity and self-worth.

So again, it wasn't that Jesus was sacrificed so that God could forgive this man. It was more about helping this man begin the process of understanding that *he was worth being forgiven.* Under this understanding of the cross, God, in Jesus, willingly laid down God's own life in order to show this man and all of us how unconditionally loved we truly are. It was God's way of saying, as Brennan Manning often preaches, "I love you so utterly, so completely, so extremely, that I would literally rather die than ever be without you. There's nothing—absolutely nothing—you could ever do that would make you unacceptable or unlovable to me."

We could probably pick apart the psychology and theology of that last paragraph for a long time, and feel free to. But what I'm saying here is that there is something about this notion that "God would die for us" that is very psychologically, emotionally, and spiritually powerful and liberating for many people. In the important process of rethinking doctrines such as penal substitutionary atonement, I don't want to lose the spiritual power and depth of the concept of God's "sacrificial love" altogether. That's why the word "penal," which is about punishment, is important in the phrase "penal substitutionary atonement." I don't believe that God requires that anyone be punished, let alone tortured, in order for forgiveness to be extended to us. But I do believe that God would gladly die for us.

So you see I can say that I believe "Jesus died for me—and for all of humankind," and mean that with deep conviction. Jesus' death on the cross illustrates as graphically as anyone or anything ever could that there's nothing God won't do to show us how loved we are. There are times when I've needed to know that I'm loved this wildly, especially when I've messed up and am feeling guilty and having a hard time letting myself off some hook. But this in no way implies that I believe Jesus *had* to be slaughtered *in order for* God to forgive me or anyone else.

The Cross As God's *Way* of Overcoming Evil

Another way in which the death of Jesus on the cross holds deep meaning for me and many progressive Christians is that it reveals God's way of confronting and ultimately overcoming the power of evil. There are aspects of the Christus Victor theory in what I'm about to articulate here.

Quite simply—Jesus used what is sometimes referred to as "Lamb Power"—the paradoxical power of love that is willing to suffer and be *apparently* defeated in order to ultimately win over and even liberate an adversary or some opposing force. This is the kind of costly Love which Jesus embodied and revealed to the world.

This is the kind of "power" that Mahatma Gandhi learned from Jesus and which he used to non-violently overcome the British Empire in India. This "Lamb Power" was also employed powerfully by Dr. Martin Luther King, Jr. during the civil rights movement in the United States. It's the opposite of "kicking butt for Jesus" or for anyone or anything else.

This kind of power is not passive or weak. Neither is it violent or coercive.

To me this is profoundly important. There have been and continue to be too many attempts historically to somehow see Jesus as a macho, militaristic figure in whose name nations or churches can "win something" or "take something back" for God.

This understanding of Jesus as one who "kicked butt for God's sake" is what some people have referred to as the "Rambo Jesus."

It is at the heart of what author and scholar Walter Wink so aptly coined, "the Myth of Redemptive Violence."

This myth, which Walter Wink explores powerfully in his books (I suggest The Powers That Be[7] for the most succinct overview), is basically the whole notion that "might makes right."

Wink makes a very compelling case that this Myth of Redemptive Violence is really the official religion of the American Empire. He claims that the primary "catechism" of this American religion of redemptive violence is Saturday morning cartoons!

I can relate. I'm dating myself here, but I grew up watching the cartoon character Popeye eat his spinach so he could find his butt kicking mojo and beat the you know what out of his nemesis Bluto. That show used to make my blood boil! I can remember the downright lust for "redemptive violence" that those cartoons caused to make rage within my little red blooded American boy's body. By the time Popeye finally got to that can of spinach I was practically beside myself with a desire to see Bluto get righteously destroyed.

After all, Popeye was the good guy, and Bluto had it coming.

And isn't this the "juice" behind just about every action movie plot, every cop TV show, and just about every attempt to sell a foreign policy of going to war?

Some bad person or enemy or nation or group always seems to "have it coming." It's okay to use extreme force to beat the bad or evil people into submission—or so we believers in the myth of redemptive violence always claim.

But didn't Jesus tell us to "love our enemies?" It's amazing how skilled we are at figuring out ways not to "hear" that teaching, let alone take it seriously enough to attempt to live it out.

This idea of righteous violence is so deeply ingrained in most of us that it's hard for us to even consider the true power of Jesus' non-violent and radically loving methodology for confronting, disarming, and ultimately overcoming the power of violence and injustice in this world.

If you'd like to read more about "Lamb Power" and God's overcoming evil in and through the power of sacrificial love, I highly recommend a book by Shane Claiborne and Chris Haw called Jesus For President.[8] They brilliantly explore this theme and many others closely related to it. The following quote, which I find pretty amusing, is from this book on page 194. These words were uttered by a pastor named Mark Driscoll and were originally published in *Relevant Magazine (January-February 2007)*. They are a great expression of the Rambo Jesus mentality;

> *Some emergent types want to recast Jesus as a limp-wrist hippie in a dress with a lot of product in His hair, who drank decaf and made pithy Zen statements about life while shopping for the perfect pair of shoes. In Revelation, Jesus is a prize fighter with a tattoo down His leg, a sword in His hand and the commitment to make someone bleed. That is a guy I can worship. I cannot worship the hippie, diaper, halo Christ because I cannot worship a guy I can beat up.*

Progressive Christians reject the notion of the Rambo Jesus. Violent, militaristic imagery will rarely be used in Progressive Christian Worship Music. We reject what is often referred to as "Christian triumphalism."

Yes, Jesus "exposed and defeated" the powers of evil. But his only "weapons" were Love and Truth and his own willingness to suffer and even die for others—including those who opposed him—and those who put nails through his hands and feet. He refused any and all attempts to use military might or any other form of worldly might in order to overcome enemies and impose the Divine will. This is not about Jesus being "a wimp." It's about redefining what true strength—the strength of Love—is all about.

THE CROSS AS THE COST OF SPEAKING TRUTH TO POWER

The point here is simply that progressive Christians find lots of meaning in the "prophetic" interpretation of the cross as well. This explanation of why Jesus was crucified tends to fall into the "Moral Exemplar" theory mentioned by Tony Jones.

According to this understanding, Jesus spoke truth to the religious and political powers in first century Palestine, and was therefore regarded to be a threat to the status quo. He did not call for violent revolution, but he challenged the hypocrisy of the established religious authorities, and when he overturned the tables in the temple, he challenged the whole religious and economic machine at the heart of religious and political power in Jerusalem.

As it's often put, Jesus "spoke Truth to power in Love."

He spoke out on behalf of the poor, and challenged the privilege and power of the wealthy. So the "powers that be" got together and conspired to do away with him, just as they do in any historical context to prophets whose clear voices and positions represent a threat to the systems which are built upon injustice, inequity, greed, and dishonesty.

When threatened strongly enough, the established powers and authorities will ultimately kill those who stand for love and justice and compassion. The history of the Church is full of faithful and courageous men and women who were put to death for following Jesus' example in this regard. Dietrich Bonhoeffer, Oscar Romero, and Martin Luther King Jr. are recent examples of Christians put to death for challenging the established powers. There are countless other women and men whose names we will never know—at least not on this side of the grave.

Jesus—who paid the ultimate price for being a loving but strong champion of the poor and advocate for justice—will be very present in Progressive Christian Worship Music.

THE CROSS AS PART OF THE PATTERN OF DEATH AND RENEWAL

Another way in which the cross of Jesus is deeply meaningful to me is because it helps reveal a pattern of sorts that is woven into the very fabric of the universe itself. I'm talking here about the processes of death and renewal through which growth and transformation happens. Once we begin to recognize this pattern, we see it everywhere. It's in the rhythm of the seasons. The vital lush life of summer gives way to the "death" of fall and winter, and then the renewal of spring, and then back into new the life and growth of summer. This is how creation itself progresses, and this is how humans also grow—physically, emotionally, and spiritually. Every cell in our bodies dies and is replaced by new cells. I've been told that within a seven year period, all the cells in our bodies are replaced and we are literally "new beings."

Theologically, this pattern is classically referred to as "the paschal mystery." I'll spare you too much detail about the origins of this term, but suffice it to say that it's all about this pattern of death and resurrection. I don't want to in any way romanticize or spiritualize the agony of Jesus' death on the cross. It was a horrific experience of capital punishment through torture. But the point here is that death is not the final word. The agony of Good Friday was what preceded the incredibly joyful surprise of Easter Sunday. The paschal mystery is all about how grief, loss, and excruciating pain so often leads to joy, learning, new life, fresh insights, and transformation.

As is so often the case for me, no one articulates the deep truths of this pattern better than Fr. Richard Rohr, who wrote;

> *Paul spoke of "reproducing the pattern" of his death and thus understanding resurrection (Phil. 3:11). That teaching will never fail. The soul is always freed and formed in such wisdom. Native religions speak of winter and summer; mystical authors speak of darkness and light; Eastern religion speaks of yin and yang or the Tao. Seasons transform the year; light and darkness transform the day. Christians call it the paschal mystery, but we are all pointing to the necessity of both descent and ascent.*

> *The paschal mystery is the pattern of transformation. We are transformed through death and rising, probably many times. There seems to be no other cauldron of growth and transformation.*

> *We seldom go freely into the belly of the beast. Unless we face a major disaster like the death of a friend or spouse or loss of a marriage or job, we usually will not go there. As a culture, we have to be taught the language of descent. That is the great language of religion. It teaches us to enter willingly, trustingly into the dark periods of life. These dark periods are good teachers. Religious energy is in the dark questions, seldom in the answers. Answers are the way out. Answers are not what we are here for. When we look for answers, we're looking to change the pattern. When we look at the questions, we look for the opening to transformation. The good*

energy is all in the questions, seldom in the answers. Fixing something doesn't usually transform us. We try to change events in order to avoid changing ourselves. Instead we must learn to stay with the pain of life, without answers, without conclusions, and some days without meaning. That is the path, the perilous dark path of true prayer.[9]

Jesus told his disciples at several points throughout the gospels that following him will involve "taking up their own crosses" (Matthew 16:24). He was letting them and us know that while living in the Way of Jesus will involve times of pain and suffering (as will life itself), the pain we experience will lead us into new life and joy and growth if we are willing to let that be the case. The cross leads to resurrection. As professor, author, and evangelist Tony Campolo often puts it, "It's Friday, but Sunday's coming." That's the pattern.

This understanding of the cross has helped me many times when I've been in the midst of something difficult. I'm reminded that God, in Christ, knows what it's like to be in pain. And I'm reminded that if I stay with it, the pain will eventually pass and something beautiful will emerge as a result. This can sound trite if it's reduced to some pious platitude and thrown at someone who is hurting terribly when he or she is not ready to hear it. But it can be a profound source of comfort and strength and wisdom when we live our way into the depths of this pattern.

This theme of new life that comes out of suffering and pain will certainly be part of the theology which is at the heart of Progressive Christian Worship Music.

I WAS THERE WHEN THEY CRUCIFIED MY CHRIST

Yes, that was an inclusive quote of the old spiritual, "Were You There When They Crucified My *Lord?*"

I don't believe that Jesus had to be sacrificed in order for God to forgive our sins.

But I do believe that Jesus went to the cross *because* of our sins.

By "our," I'm referring to humankind.

No, of course neither you nor I were literally "there" when Jesus was crucified.

But in a general sense, it was human sin that put Jesus on that cross. The fear, pride, envy, selfishness, stubbornness, and lust for power that led the Pharisees, scribes, and Roman authorities to kill Jesus are representative of the fear, pride, envy, etc.—the sin—that is in all of us.

In some mystical sense which I'll never be able to adequately explain, I believe that God was in Jesus, on the cross, absorbing into God's own being all the wrongs of all people that have ever been committed or ever will be committed.

He didn't do this because he had to in order for us to be acceptable to God. Christ did it because God loves us and wants us to know that there are often severe consequences for choosing against the ways of Love.

We can't kid ourselves about this.

As Dr. James Loder, a professor of mine at seminary once said during a lecture which I've remembered for close to thirty years now;

> It's kind of like spiritual mathematics; two negatives equal a positive; on the cross, Jesus negated all the things that negate life. He put an end to the things that put an end to us. It's as if Jesus was hanging on the cross saying to us, 'Don't you see what you are doing to yourselves? Don't you see how much you hurt yourselves by living this way? This is what happens when you reject Truth and Love—you bring about suffering and death. What you're doing to me on this cross—this is what you're doing to yourselves, to the human race, and to all of creation.'

I don't know if that's helpful to you or not, but it's meaningful to me. I'm probably not much different from most folks, but the truth is I've made plenty of mistakes in my life. I've rejected God and God's Truth and intention for my life countless times—usually quietly and privately, and usually without fully realizing it and without malice.

But there have been times when my rejections of God's will have been reckless and foolish and deliberate. Times when I knew better. In those times, I rejected the "Light that came into this world (John 3:19)." In those times, in a very personal spiritual sense, I was among those who turned their backs on Jesus, and I was among those whose "sins" sent Jesus to the cross.

Some of what I'm trying to articulate here will probably sound over the top to many of my progressive Christian friends, but I think it's important to be real about the consequences of the selfishness which can sometimes cause us to make choices to do things that we never dreamed we'd be capable of doing. Maybe it's only those of us who have really messed up who will get this. I count myself among this number. I'll just leave it there.

But one of the reasons why I'm so drawn to Jesus and to his way of knowing and embodying God's love is that the God of Jesus takes sin—"missing the mark"—and evil very seriously. I'm talking about the sinful acts and choices of individuals here, but also about the brokenness and mess of this entire world—all its people and all of its systems and structures—for all time.

I've lived long enough and traveled widely enough to know that as beautiful as life is, this world is also full of incredible suffering and cruelty. Much of it is attributable to human sin. I'm drawn to the whole story of Jesus as the "Savior" of the world because it seems painfully obvious that individual persons and this broken world all need some "saving." The root of the biblical word "salvation" by the way is the same root for the word "salve." In other words, it's more about healing and restoration to wholeness than rescue or escape.

To me, Jesus beautifully embodied and reveals the Way, the Truth, and the Life that leads to healing and wholeness and transformation of individual persons and also of this world. For individuals, this Way involves a process of acknowledging and owning our own sinful acts and choices and the painful consequences of those choices. We do this not to beat ourselves up, but to honestly recognize and deal with our own capacity to miss the mark. Then we can let God's amazing grace remind us that we are loved unconditionally, pick up the pieces, learn from our mistakes, and keep learning, growing, and working to make God's Dream for the world a present reality.

Moving Toward A Conclusion

Well, if you've read this entire chapter, congratulations and thank you for hanging in there! I know I threw a lot at you. But as I said at the beginning, I felt like I owed you some depth. I have no doubt that some readers will be troubled by all of this questioning of penal substitutionary atonement, and for that reason I wanted to help you understand how I and many other progressive Christians still find life-transforming and world-healing meaning in the cross of Jesus Christ.

If it came across as self-indulgent on my part to invite you to journey through some of this theology with me, well, my apologies, and thanks for reading in any case.

But I hope and pray this chapter also helped you realize that even though we are choosing not to emphasize doctrines like penal substitutionary atonement in Progressive Christian Worship Music, there is still so much deep, joyful, gutsy theological truth and meaning for progressive Christians to celebrate and to write and sing about!

I also hope I've made it very clear that proponents and creators of Progressive Christian Worship Music have no agenda to somehow tell people for whom doctrines such as penal substitutionary atonement are central that they must abandon their beliefs in any way. If that doctrine speaks to your heart and rings true to your soul, by all means embrace it. I will not love or respect or desire to work with you on behalf of God's intentions any less!

Finally, let me just own once more that the thoughts and opinions expressed in this chapter are primarily my own. I think many progressive Christians will resonate with lots of what I've written, but I am not trying to speak for others or to create some kind of progressive orthodoxy. My intention has simply been to help you understand some of the deeper reasons why progressive Christians don't tend to find the doctrine of PSA to be compelling, and why you won't find it promoted in and through the worship music we create.

Chapter 12: Questions For Discussion

1. You already had a chance to discuss the doctrine of penal substitutionary atonement during the discussion of chapter 3, but after reading this chapter, is there anything more about this doctrine that you'd like to explore with each other?

2. There were six sections in this chapter which mentioned ways in which Bryan and many other progressive Christians find deep meaning in the cross of Jesus, even without embracing penal substitutionary atonement. Those six sections were:

   1. The End of Sacrificial Killing (The Last Scapegoat)
   2. The Psychological Power of the Cross
   3. The Cross As God's Way of Overcoming Evil
   4. The Cross As the Cost of Speaking Truth to Power
   5. The Cross as Part of the Pattern of Death and Renewal
   6. I Was There When They Crucified My Christ

   Were any of these concepts particularly meaningful to you? Disturbing? Share some of your thoughts about the ideas explored in these sections with each other.

4. You have now completed the actual content of this book. What about this overall book has been most helpful or meaningful to you?

5. How will reading and discussing this book impact your music ministry?

6. Close with a time of prayer, asking God to guide your music ministry and to give you a deep passion for helping your congregation to worship God in song.

CHAPTER 13

Some Closing Thoughts and Invitations

It's a vulnerable thing to put one's most cherished beliefs and opinions into words and "send them out there" for the world to read. It's even more vulnerable when you know that some of what is written is most likely going to be controversial. And it's a bit daunting when you also know that most people who question more conservative ways of understanding doctrine and Scripture tend to be rather ruthlessly attacked and taken to task by those who regard their positions as a threat to Christian orthodoxy.

So I'm bracing myself a bit.

Then again, this book will only be potentially controversial if folks actually read it—and at this point I have no idea if anyone will!

So if you're finishing this book, I'm so grateful for your time and energy. If you find yourself disturbed by my reflections in any way, just know that I'm approachable and open to communicating with you. If you love God, Christ, Jesus, God's Dream for the world, and biblical truth, the things that you and I have in common are way more important than anything that could possibly divide us.

If reading this book has somehow helped you to think more deeply about the words of the songs you sing as you worship God, then it was worth the time and energy it has taken me to write it. If it has helped you to deepen your faith and clarify your own theology and beliefs, I'm delighted and profoundly grateful.

And if this book has provided a way for you and your pastor and your music ministry team to discuss your ministry, get to know each other better, be more deliberate about the purpose and content and quality of the music you choose for worship, do some of the reflection and ego work that we all need to do in the process of ministering, and sing your faith with more passion, joy, and integrity—then I have accomplished what I set out to do, and I'm humbled and grateful beyond words to be a part of this process.

JOIN THE SHIFT!

As was stated in the introduction, one of my goals in writing this book was to try to help shift the tone and focus of the conversation that so often takes place in mainline churches when it comes to "contemporary praise and worship music." Too often that conversation is about complaining about what more progressive folks don't like about the language and theology of this music.

So let's shift the conversation! Let's focus on bringing into being the music that we are longing to find and sing in our churches. Let's help each other find it, create it, and get it "out there." Let's encourage the musicians and composers in our churches to start creating music that will help their congregations sing their hearts out to God in musical styles and language and theology that truly fits our congregations.

In 2010, I contacted three musicians whose music I love and whose theology I trust and suggested that we work together to create opportunities for progressive musicians and pastors to do all the things to which I just referred. I've mentioned all three of these songwriter/theologian/ musicians in the course of this book. They are Christopher Grundy, Richard Bruxvoort-Colligan, and Andra Moran. Together, the four of us have designed a retreat model which we are calling SHIFT.

Our first retreat took place in the summer of 2011 at a beautiful United Church of Christ retreat center in Green Lake, WI called Pilgrim Center. In fact that camp's director at the time, Jeff Puhlmann-Becker (and his entire family for that matter), was also instrumental in offering the space, hospitality, and administrative oversight that made this initial SHIFT retreat possible. It wouldn't have happened without Jeff's incredibly gifted leadership.

About fifty progressive Christian musicians and pastors throughout the country gathered for that first three and a half day SHIFT retreat. It was a profoundly inspiring and transforming event for those who attended, and at the end of it we realized that some kind of movement had been birthed during our time together.

SHIFT will continue to offer this summer retreat annually, and we have also developed a model for a weekend retreat that will take place in other regions of the country. You can find out more about this movement and these regional retreats by visiting the SHIFT website www.shiftmusic. org. Please consider yourself to be enthusiastically invited to join us and perhaps even to host a retreat in your region. The Spirit is up to something powerful here! Let's help bring this new genre of worship music into being together.

In addition to SHIFT, we have established a Facebook page called PCAN—Progressive Christian Artists Network. This network is open to other progressive Christian artists whose art may be visual, dance, written, etc. Artists of all types are welcome. Let's find each other, promote each other's work when appropriate, and encourage each other in whatever ways we can. If you're a progressive Christian artist of some kind, please let us know who you are and let's continue this conversation together.

The SHIFT leadership team is also in the process of establishing a website through which our individual music and related resources will be available for purchase, and we'll be doing some writing and recording together as well. That website is not quite up and running as I write this, so please be in touch with me or Christopher, Andra, or Richard to find out more about this online "store" in the future.

CHAPTER 14

Sources of Progressive Christian Worship Music

One of the things that I'm very excited about is helping folks to find sources of Progressive Christian Worship Music. The truth is that I'm really not aware of many composers who are deliberately creating the kind of music which this book describes.

But I'm sure there are many more folks out there writing these kinds of songs than I know about.

So please, by all means contact me and let me know about music and songwriters whom I've yet to come across. It is very much my intention to create an easy way for churches to find great sources of Progressive Christian Worship Music, and publishing and distributing this music is part of what my company and ministry are all about.

At this point, the following are the best sources of Progressive Christian Worship Music with which I'm currently familiar. I've listed myself first, and then the rest of the folks mentioned are in no particular order . . .

1. **Bryan Sirchio and Crosswind Music:** Yes, this is my own publishing company through which I make my music available. I'm listing myself first because hey—I wrote the book! But I'm not claiming that my material is better than any others listed. We've all got our own styles and strengths.

You can find my music for all ages on my website www.bryansirchio.com, and also at www.progressivechristianmusic.com and at **www.6marks.com**

You can also reach me and order my music toll free at **1-800-735-0850.**

On my website you'll find recordings and songbooks for young children (great for Sunday Schools and children's choirs), teens (along with study guides that turn each song into a youth group or confirmation class study session), solo albums for adults that feature progressive theology, and sheet music that is downloadable. My music is also available on i-Tunes, Napster, Rhapsody, and Amazon.

I've recently released a collection of Progressive Christian Worship Music called **"Something Beautiful For God."**

It features **24 songs written for congregational singing**, and I've put together a package which makes it very easy to bring this music into the life of a congregation.

The package includes:

- a **songbook with piano arrangements** for all 24 songs, as well as guitar lead sheet arrangements with guitar chord diagrams. There are also "lyric and chord" sheets for each song, and a split track CD in the book with the piano accompaniment on one side of the stereo field and the acoustic guitar accompaniment on the other side. This enables pianists and guitarists to hear what the music is supposed to sound like.

- a **CD of all 24 songs fully produced with vocals** the way I'd do them with a worship band in church.

- an **accompaniment track CD with all 24 songs with vocals removed** so that congregations that don't have a band can sing to the fully produced music.

- a **CD with the lyrics of all songs in Word files and PowerPoint** with images for projection. This CD also **includes PDF files of bulletin insert lead sheets** so that worshippers can have musical notation for all of the songs.

  You can find out more about this package and order it online by visiting my website www.bryansirchio.com.

- Individual songs can be downloaded as MP3s on my site or on I-tunes, and sheet music for individual songs can also be purchased and downloaded immediately.

- Feel free to call toll free to order or if you have questions: **1-800-735-0850.** The entire package described costs $59 plus $6 postage, but any of the items can be purchased individually as well.

2. **Sing! Prayer and Praise:** This is a new collection of over a hundred songs released by the United Church of Christ's (UCC's) Publishing House under the leadership of Rev. Scott Ressman. An excellent committee worked hard to choose songs that meet the 6 marks of Progressive Christian Worship Music. They did not have these 6 marks before them as I have specifically articulated them, but the committee was formed precisely to create a source of new "praise music" for UCC churches (and other more progressive congregations) with theology and language that mainline and more progressive pastors and members can feel good about. These songbooks can be purchased by visiting the UCC's website and following the appropriate links www.ucc.org.

3. **Christopher Grundy:** Dr. Christopher Grundy is an ordained UCC minister and also a Professor of Liturgical Arts and Preaching at Eden Theological Seminary outside St. Louis, MO. He has recorded several CDs and released a songbook. In the Spring of 2012 he released a collection of songs for congregational worship called "Stepping In," and it's really wonderful. I always refer to Christopher as one of the finest composers of new music in the Church today. He has a profound gift for writing beautiful choruses that are musically and theologically compelling, yet very easy to learn and sing. I'm really

excited to see Christopher's music more widely distributed and used. In addition to his liturgical music, he has also released several solo "singer/songwriter" albums that progressive Christians will love. You can purchase his music at www.christophergrundy.com, and 10 of his songs are also in the "Sing! Prayer and Praise" collection.

4. **Richard Bruxvoort-Colligan:** Much of Richard's ministry has unfolded in ELCA Lutheran Church contexts. Richard writes beautiful liturgical music that easily fit the criteria of "Progressive Christian Worship Music." He has released a wonderful new Lenten series of liturgies and music, as well as songs that are born out of time Richard has spent lingering with the Psalms. A number of Richard's songs are also in the "Sing! Prayer and Praise Collection." You can order Richard's music at www.worldmaking.net

5. **Andra Moran:** Andra's roots are in the Christian Church Disciples of Christ denomination, and she's toured extensively for the past 15 years or so with her wonderful ministry of original music. In addition to her concert bookings, she leads the music at a creative new church experiment in Nashville called "The Bridge." Andra deeply grasps all of the issues in this book and has beautiful solo material as well as some great songs written for worship. In June of 2012 she released a fantastic collection of songs for congregational singing called "Harmony Grove." She also has songs published in the "Sing! Prayer and Praise" collection and in the well known Chalice Hymnal. Purchase Andra's music at www.andramoran.com.

6. **James F.D. Martin:** Jim is a UCC pastor and composer and close friend of mine. Hymns of his are in the New Century Hymnal, and also in "Sing! Prayer and Praise." Jim has released several CDs of songs and you can reach him through his website: www.blendedworshipresources. com.

7. **Brian D. McLaren:** Brian is a prominent Christian pastor, author, activist and speaker and leading figure in the emerging church movement. He is also a very gifted songwriter and has released a collection of songs called, "Songs For A Revolution of Hope, Vol. 1." You can find out more about this music by going to the following link:

http://brianmclaren.bandcamp.com/album/songs-for-a-revolution-of-hope.

8. **Aaron Niequist:** I've just recently discovered Aaron's music, and I'm rapidly becoming a fan. So far one of my favorite songs of his is, "Love Can Change The World." Aaron was a worship leader at Mars Hill church in Grand Rapids, MI when Rob Bell was there, and he now is on the staff of Willow Creek Church outside Chicago. You can listen to his music at www.aaronniequist.com. If you come from the mainline church end of the progressive Christian movement, prepare to have some of your assumptions about mega churches and Willow Creek blown open a bit!

9. **Newer Hymnals such as the UCC's New Century Hymnal:** This new hymnal sparked all kinds of controversy when it was being compiled and first released precisely because the editors were very much focused on making sure that the lyrics of the hymns had the kind of theological and linguistic integrity and inclusiveness that this book is about. They did not use my "6 marks of Progressive Christian Music" as a guide of course, but their priorities and sensibilities were very similar. One reason why this hymnal was so controversial though is because the editors took liberties to rewrite and alter many of the lyrics of hymns that have been sung and cherished for centuries. Some folks either miss the older original version of the songs (especially things like Christmas hymns that have such sentimental and/or theological power for many), or they dislike the newer words. You can't please everyone! But this compilation was and is a very bold and effective attempt to make the traditional hymnody of the church more consistent with the kind of theology that Progressive Christians can embrace. And, in addition to the old beloved hymns there are quite a few new hymns which are beautiful and which have wonderful theology.

10. **Jeff Lowery:** Jeff is an ordained deacon in the United Methodist Church who has written some beautiful songs for worship that reflect the 6 Marks of Progressive Christian Worship Music. He has released one CD and has sheet music available for a number of his congregational compositions. He can be contacted at www.jefflowerymusic.com.

11. **Dakota Road Music:** Dakota Road features the music of Larry Olson and Hans Peterson. They are best known in ELCA Lutheran circles. I have not listened to enough of their music to know if they would "line up" consistently with all of the six marks, but I know that they are theologically very intentional about earth keeping, social justice, and many other themes that progressive Christians would appreciate. They have an extensive catalogue and all kinds of resources that can be found on their website www.dakotaroadmusic.com

12. **Sara Kay:** Sara Kay is a singer/songwriter with a beautiful voice who is very conscious of and deliberate about progressive theology and inclusive language her music. To the best of my knowledge she has not created an album primarily of congregational songs, but some of the tunes on her "On The Way" recording could be used for group worship. I have no doubt that she will create and release some good Progressive Christian Worship Music in the years to come. At this point the best way to connect with her would be on Facebook.

13. **Troy Bronsink:** Troy is a passionate and extremely creative singer/songwriter who lives in Cincinnati, OH. He has just released a wonderful collection of songs called "Songs to Pray By" which I encourage you to check out. You can find Troy on Facebook or on his website www.churchasart.com.

14. **Ken Medema:** I would imagine that most of you know of Ken! He's been around a while sharing his amazing gifts, and he just keeps cranking out beautiful and soulful projects, so be sure to see what he's got to offer these days. Find him at www.kenmedema.com.

15. **John van de Laar:** John is a Methodist pastor, author, and songwriter from South Africa. He's got a wonderful website full of excellent songs and resources. www.sacredise.com.

16. **Jonathan Rundman:** I am brand new to Jonathan and his music, but my friend Richard Bruxvoort-Colligan raves about Jonathan and refers to him as an extremely gifted writer, theologian, and performer. So I encourage you to check out what he has to offer at www.jonathanrundman.com.

17. **Emily Helin Olson**: Emily is a wonderful musician and worship leader with extensive experience in contemporary worship music. She is an MA graduate of Luther Seminary, St. Paul MN, and has ministered with congregations in a number of denominations, including the Presbyterian Church USA, the Evangelical Lutheran Church in America, the United Methodist Church, the Baptist General Conference, and the United Church of Christ. Emily understands the nuances of progressive worship and Progressive Christian Worship Music. She is beginning a consulting business through which she will be available to come to congregations, meet with their worship music teams, and help them develop a plan for transforming their worship, determining what kind of worship music is appropriate for that congregation, and coaching worship musicians in the process of bringing new styles of music into their worship. You can contact Emily via e-mail at edholson@gmail.com.

ENDNOTES

1. The "C" in "Church" is usually capitalized when referring to the Church throughout the world. I recently read Philip Gulley's book If The Church Were Christian, and in it he suggests that this use of this capital "C" seems a bit presumptuous to him. I've decided to keep the traditional "C," but I must admit that every time I read it now I think of Philip Gulley's perspective and am reminded of the Church's arrogance at countless points in history.

2. This address was given at the Annual Meeting of the Wisconsin Conference of the United Church of Christ. I am drawing from it from memory, so I may have gotten a detail slightly off here and there, but the essence of the story is accurate.

3. For a really nice and succinct exploration of gender issues as they relate to some of Jesus' teachings, check out Walter Wink's The Powers That Be.

4. Google "El Shaddai and the breasted one" and you'll find many references to explain and back this up, including Wikipedia.

Chapter Three

1. Robert H. Bell Jr., *Love Wins: A Book About Heaven, Hell, and the Fate of Every Person Who Ever Lived*, (New York, NY, HarperCollins Publishers, 2011).

2. Rev. Nadia Bolz-Weber is pastor of The House For All Sinners and Saints in Denver, CO. This sermon was called, "Maundy Thursday At House For All Sinners and Saints." It was preached on April 6, 2012 and can be found at the following link: http://www.patheos.

com/blogs/nadiabolzweber/2012/04/http://www.patheos.com/blogs/
nadiabolzweber/2012/04/.

3. Eric Elnes, *The Phoenix Affirmations: A New Vision for the Future of Christianity*, (San Francisco, CA, Jossey-Bass, 2006). See chapter one on "Affirmation One," pp.3 and following.

Chapter Four

1. This song is on my "Something Beautiful For God" collection, and can be purchased or downloaded on my website www.bryansirchio. com. I've put together a comprehensive package of materials that make it easy to introduce these songs to congregations. You can read more about it in the final chapter of this book. Sheet music is also available on my website as an individual song or as part of the "Something Beautiful For God" songbook. This song is also available on I-tunes.

Chapter Five

1. This quote is from a blog post on December 27, 2011 called "20 Years Without A Drink: It's Personal." http://www.patheos.com/blogs/ nadiabolzweber/2011/12/20-years-without-a-drink-its-personal/ Nadia's blog is one of my most consistent sources of spiritual inspiration. Her blog is called "Sarcastic Lutheran: the cranky spirituality of a postmodern gal."

2. The exact wording of this well known quote is "God created man in his image, and man returned the compliment." I changed "man" to "human" to make this language more inclusive. I have tried extensively to find out exactly where Pascal wrote this, but have not been able to locate the source, even though the quote is widely used. In fact, in slightly altered forms it has also been attributed to Twain, Voltaire, Shaw, and Rousseau! I remain convinced that the French mathematician and philosopher Blaise Pascal was the original source of this quote, as numerous others have attributed it to him.

Chapter Six

1. Richard is a good friend of mine and a wonderful singer/songwriter. You can listen to this song on his website www.worldmaking.net. The URL http://www.worldmaking.net/ground-and-source.php will take you right to this song. Richard is also one of the founding members of The SHIFT movement along with Christopher Grundy, Andra Moran, and me www.shiftmusic.org.

2. Smith, James K. A., <u>Desiring the Kingdom: Worship, Worldview and Cultural Formation</u> (Grand Rapids: Baker Academic, 2009), p.54.

3. I've never met Derek, but I have a lot of respect for his music. Good old Google will give you plenty of opportunities to familiarize yourself with his ministry and to see the entire lyric of this song (which is more of a solo song than a worship song). Derek's website is www.derekwebb.com. He was a member of a well known Christian band named Caedman's Call before launching his solo career. Given the fact that he comes out of the more conservative Contemporary Christian Music industry, he has been courageous in the themes of his songs, and has taken plenty of criticism for (among other things) challenging Christians to be more loving toward the GLBT community.

4. Christopher gave this lecture at First Congregational Church in Rockford, IL in 2005 at the annual meeting of the Prairie Association of the UCC. He then clarified these remarks for me in subsequent conversations. Dr. Grundy is a close personal friend of mine and fantastic singer/songwriter. His music can be found at www.christophergrundy.com.

5. Brian K. Blount & Leonora Tubbs Tisdale, *Making Room at the Table: An Invitation to Multicultural Worship,* (Louisville, KY, Westminster John Knox Press, 2001).

6. "Here In This Place" is on Christopher's "Come to the Feast" CD and songbook. You can purchase it on Christopher's website www.christophergrundy.com.

Chapter Seven

1. van de Laar, John (2010-10-28). <u>The Hour That Changes Everything</u> (Kindle Location 368). Sacredise. Kindle Edition.

2. van de Laar, John (2010-10-28). <u>The Hour That Changes Everything</u> (Kindle Locations 490-497). Sacredise. Kindle Edition.

3. This is not to suggest in any way that only Christians or those who embrace the Bible "truly worship." But since this book is about Progressive *Christian* Worship Music, then group worship for Christians will most often involve some reading and responding to the Judeo-Christian scriptures. Worship of the kind that I am describing however certainly *could* involve drawing from Divine Truths found in other sacred texts and religions as well.

4. Gordon Cosby is the founding pastor of the well known "Church of The Saviour" in Washington, D.C. I have been privileged to know him and serve on a board of directors with him, and this is a phrase he often used in his preaching and teaching.

5. Andra Moran is an exceptionally gifted singer/songwriter who comes out of the Disciples of Christ tradition. She is also one of the founders of the SHIFT movement along with Christopher Grundy, Richard Bruxvoort-Colligan, and me. She has just released a new project of worship songs called, "Harmony Grove." You can find her at www. andramoran.com.

6. You can find this article at www.farsipraise.net/cgi-bin/**articles**/3-10-2005—17-19-52_**article**.pdf

7. van de Laar, John (2010-10-28). <u>The Hour That Changes Everything</u> (Kindle Locations 354-363). Sacredise. Kindle Edition.

Chapter 8

1. Dr. Peter J. Gomes was dean at Harvard Divinity School and a faculty member at Harvard as well. He was one of the featured speakers at

the General Synod of the UCC in 2007 in Hartford, CT. This was the UCC's 50th anniversary. Dr. Gomes passed away in March, 2011. I have attempted to find a transcript or video of this address, but have been unsuccessful thus far. I was privileged to be present to hear this address and am citing this remark from memory. I believe that a video of this message exists, and I will continue to try to locate it. Please feel free to contact me to see if I have been able to find it. This address is definitely worth listening to.

Chapter 9

[1.] Dr. Grundy made this statement at his lecture at First Congregational Church in Rockford, IL in 2005 at the annual meeting of the Prairie Association of the UCC.

Chapter 10

[1.] Rev. Bob Wang can be reached at bwang4@wi.rr.com. If for some reason this e-mail is no longer current when you attempt to reach him, please just contact me and I'll let you know his current contact information. Andra Moran www.andramoran.com would also be a great person to consult with regarding praise and worship songs that are useful in more progressive Christian worship circles.

Chapter 11

[1.] Dr. Karl Kuhn shared this overview of The Function of Scripture in Christian Tradition at the Annual Meeting of the Wisconsin Conference of the United Church of Christ in June, 2012. He is a brilliant and faithful scholar and beloved professor of religion at Lakeland College, Sheboygan, WI. He graciously granted me permission to include this overview in this book.

[2.] Sara Miles, *Take This Bread: A Radical Conversion*, (New York, NY, Ballantine Books, 2007).

[3.] Richard Rohr, *The Naked Now: Learning to See as the Mystics See*, (New York, NY, The Crossroad Publishing Company, 2009).

4. Henri J.M. Nouwen, *The Wounded Healer: Ministry in Contemporary Society*, (New York, NY, Image Book/Doubleday, 1972).

5. Richard Rohr's teachings and remarks come to us as much through his recorded live addresses as through his books. This remark of his was from a recording I heard years ago and which I no longer have, and I cannot remember the address in which I heard Fr. Rohr say this. Obviously it struck me deeply. I contacted Fr. Rohr's organization and was granted permission to include this remark and to attribute it to Fr. Rohr. His exact words may have been slightly different, but he agrees that the essence of the comment is accurate.

6. This quote which I'm attributing to Will Rogers has been attributed to several others as well; Mark Twain, and early American humorists Artemus Ward and Henry Wheeler Shaw (aka Josh Billings) have also been given credit for this quote. And nowhere is the original source offered! At least not that I've found yet.

Chapter 12

1. The wonderful Nadia Bolz-Weber was the source of this remark in her June 11, 2012 sermon called "A Re-telling of Adam and Eve and That Damned Snake." http://www.patheos.com/blogs/nadiabolzweber/

2. Tony Jones, *A Better Atonement: Beyond the Depraved Doctrine of Original Sin*, (Minneapolis, MN, The JoPa Group, 2012). 5

3. Jones, page not listed because this book is in e-book format and no page numbers are given. It is in Part Two, and in the section called "Better Atonements."

4. Jones, Part Two, in the section called "Substitution, Without The Penal."

5. This is another saying of Richard Rohr's that I am quoting from a recorded address of his that I heard but cannot cite exactly. I have contacted Richard Rohr and he agrees that this quote is accurate. And obviously, being the incredibly articulate person he is, he was being

playful in his use of the word "gooder" and is well aware that no such word actually exists!

6. Brennan Manning, *The Ragamuffin Gospel,* (Sisters, OR, Multnomah Publishers, Inc., 1990). You can read this account at http://www.tentmaker.org/reviews/ragamuffin.htm

7. Walter Wink, *The Powers That Be: Theology for a New Millennium,* (New York, NY, A Galilee Book, Published by Doubleday, 1998).

8. Shane Claiborne and Chris Haw, *Jesus For President: Politics for Ordinary Radicals,* (Grand Rapids, MI, Zondervan, 2008).

9. Richard Rohr, *Everything Belongs: The Gift of Contemplative Prayer,* (New York, NY, Crossroad Publishing Company, 2003). You can find this text online at http://terce.me/2010/08/03/richard-rohr-on-being-in-the-darkness/

ABOUT THE AUTHOR

Rev. Bryan Sirchio is a graduate of Duke University and Princeton Theological Seminary. He is an ordained minister in the United Church of Christ and served as solo pastor of two small northern Wisconsin congregations for four years in the mid 1980's. In 1987 Bryan began a freelance itinerant musical ministry which he refers to as Crosswind Music. He travels extensively throughout the U.S. and beyond offering concerts of his original music, leading worship services, offering retreats, and providing musical workshops and keynote addresses for regional and national denominational conferences.

Rev. Sirchio has published over 200 songs, released 13 albums, 4 songbooks, and 3 study guides which turn many of his songs into youth group, confirmation, and adult Christian Education curricula. His compositions have been recorded by several other artists, used in denominational videos, and featured in various songbooks and Christian education publications.

Most of Bryan's musical ministry unfolds within "mainline Protestant" circles, and in some Roman Catholic parishes as well. Bryan plays guitar and piano and has released original solo music for young children, teens, and adults. He writes in many different musical styles, depending upon the age group and purpose for which the music is created. He has also written numerous songs to be sung by congregations in the context of corporate worship.

In addition to his emotionally compelling and entertaining music, what distinguishes Bryan Sirchio's work from most "contemporary Christian music" is his progressive theology, inclusive language, honoring of the earth, commitment to social justice, and compassion for the poor. Rev. Sirchio is an engaging theologian, a gifted musician, and a prophetic Christian educator who possesses unique gifts for communicating biblical truth.